How to Create Your Balanced Life

Kolleen Meyer-Krikac

Kolleen Meyer-Krikac

How to Create Your Balanced Life
Copyright © 2017 by Kolleen Meyer-Krikac
Published by Kolleen Meyer-Krikac Publishing

ISBN 13: 978-0-9992849-0-2
ISBN 10: 0-9992849-0-8

Library of Congress Control Number: 2017912541

Author's Note: The names and identifying characteristics of people in this book have been changed to protect the privacy of the individuals.

Dedication

This book is dedicated to
Quinn, my best friend, my confidante, my counselor, listener,
supporter, husband and life partner,
Thank you for your love, understanding, encouragement and
support. Thank you for helping me to find balance. I love you!!

And to my son, Kennedy,
Being your mother has brought a new perspective to my life and
to finding balance. Thank you for being my teacher in so many ways.
You have shown me how to lose myself in fun, forget time, do a
variety of things, not work all the time, and so much more!
You have truly been a blessing!
I love you more than you will ever know!

Acknowledgements

There are a number of people to whom I owe thanks or this book never would have come to fruition. The first one is Aaron Davis who suggested I write a book to share my knowledge, experience and expertise with the world. Although I had dreamed of being an author as a child, it was my conversation with Aaron that brought me back to the idea. When I told him that others had said it all, he scolded me and reminded me that as a life coach I should know better, that I have a unique message to offer in my own way. Thank you for coaching me to write this book.

Fellow coach Cameron Popp was my accountability partner for this last push to complete this book that I began writing in 2008. We were both writing books and partnered up to see them through to publication. Thank you for the tips and resources you shared with me, and especially for connecting me with Cindy Conger! I can hardly wait to see your book in print!

My friend and former director of the Southeast Community College Entrepreneurship Center, Lincoln, Nebraska, Tim Mittan, told me to put my book writing on hold when I moved into the entrepreneurship program. He was right. I learned things through that experience that helped shape this book. I didn't think it would take me this long to get back to it, but you were right about the timing, Tim. I was too busy with other things back then and couldn't give the book the focus that I have been able to lately.

A big thank you to my editors, Cindy Conger and Faith Colburn, whose expertise, help and feedback was invaluable throughout this process. Cindy offered me important and useful information that I was totally unaware of as a first-time author. Thank you for meeting with me at Barnes and Noble to discuss the editing process, the steps involved, and how to prepare for publication with a time line. It was motivating to look at other book covers in the self-help section to start getting ideas for mine. Thank you to Faith for the free copy edit you offered as a prize at the Nebraska Writers' Guild Spring Conference! It was the prize I wanted to win!

My cover designer is Victorine Lieske. Thank you for your inspiration, encouragement, expertise and amazing design. I appreciate the time you took to respond to my emails and to answer my questions about self-publishing. You have been most generous with your time and knowledge and I appreciate it more than I can express.

Thank you to the Nebraska Writers' Guild for information, resources, support and encouragement. I only recently heard of the Guild and have found this organization to be one of the greatest resources for writers! I have met so many wonderful and helpful people in this group and I want to thank all of you who took time to visit with me, told me your stories about writing and publishing, and answered my questions.

Thank you to my friends and family who read my rough draft and offered honest feedback. Theresa Koeneke and Deanna Long, thank you so much for taking the time to help me fine-tune this book that had been on my mind for so long. A special thank you to my friend, Jennifer McDaniel, for taking a final look at my galley proof before it went to print. I appreciate your loaning me your fresh eyes to see what I couldn't and to be open and honest with me in your evaluation. You are truly good friends.

Thank you to my friend, Ali Schwanke for encouraging me to write this book.

Thank you to my mother, JoAnn and my brothers, Joe and Alex for allowing me to share some stories about our childhood and for your support in writing this book. I love you and am glad you are my family.

And finally, thank you to all of my clients for allowing me to be a part of your lives throughout the years. It has been a privilege to work with you. I hope you find this book to be helpful as you continue your life's journey.

Author's Note

Why did I choose to write a book about finding balance in life? I wanted to help other people who struggle with finding and maintaining balance in a chronically busy world. I am passionate about balanced living and it is something I am always striving for in my own life. I have been pretty successful at achieving a balance that works for me. I acknowledge that there is no magic "one size fits all" formula and that I have tweaked and adapted what works for me at different stages in my life.

Balance has been a constant theme in my life as far back as I can remember. Looking back, I can identify specific times when my life was out of balance and see my desperate desire to tip the scale back toward balance. Throughout the book, you will find examples of my struggles with imbalance and insights I gained as I worked through them. You will also find success stories of my clients as they used the tools I gave them to create balance in their lives.

I am a former teacher and former school counselor so I know how to teach and explain concepts. Beware that I require homework in order to get the most out of this book, so look for the exercises at the end of each chapter. I am a Licensed Professional Counselor, National Certified Counselor, Licensed Mental Health Practitioner and Certified Life Coach and have been in private practice for nearly twenty years. I offer public speaking, workshops, and presentations on creating life balance, finding meaning and purpose, and other topics related to personal and professional growth. I have helped numerous clients and I believe I can help you.

I will offer webinars and online courses, based on this book. For more information, go to my Website: http://www.balanced-life.us

Table of Contents

Chapter 1: Seeking Balance in My Own Life

"Life is a balance of holding on and letting go."
—Rumi

My sister, Kathy, died of leukemia at the age of fourteen. This created an imbalance in our family as well as within me. Her death left a huge void. I desperately tried to restore balance to our family, but as a seven-year-old child, I didn't know how. I tried anyway. I began sensing what my parents had wanted and expected from my sister, and I tried to provide that. I wanted to heal their pain in any way I could, even if it meant sacrificing parts of me.

Kathy was the oldest child and was outgoing, intelligent and interacted well with adults. She was a leader and was involved in as many activities as her illness allowed. My brother Joe, the second oldest, was an introvert and a follower. I was third and leaned toward introversion, but could switch to extroversion if necessary. Alex was a typical youngest child who used his antics to entertain, amuse, and to lighten the mood. He was bright, outgoing, athletic, and ornery, but he was the youngest, so he couldn't step up. I realized this and knew that it was up to me to attempt to fill the void, so I became more like Kathy. I became more outgoing and less introverted. I loved to learn and was already at the top of my class, so it wasn't a stretch to get good grades like she did. I related well to adults and always built relationships with my teachers. Kathy had kept newspaper clippings of the state and national spelling bees, so I followed in her footsteps by winning the local spelling contest and competing and placing in the top three at the county level nearly every year. I don't remember how many years Kathy had competed or how she finished, but I knew it was important to her, and guessed it was important to my parents as well. I participated in lots of activities, probably to make up for all that my sister wasn't able to do. I wanted my parents to be so involved with my activities that they wouldn't feel so much of the void of having only one daughter.

This all caught up to me as I reached the ages of 13 and 14 when my dad kept calling me Kathy. I grew angry and resentful that he didn't see me for who I was, but as a poor substitute for my sister. I'd worked so hard to be like her, but at that point I wanted to be loved and accepted for who I was. I had to set the record straight, to find a new balance within myself so I could be the person I was meant to be and help my family find its new balance.

My Childhood Health Scare

Two years after my sister's death, I was having horrible issues with my physical balance. I would be walking along and fall for no apparent reason. My dad attributed it to clumsiness and teased me by calling me "Grace." I also had chronic stomach aches. Mom said that they thought it was stress over the loss of my sister that progressed into an attempt to get attention. The pain increased and they could no longer write it off, so they took me to the doctor. Much to my parents' horror, the doctor told them I had a tumor. They had just lost one daughter and were terrified they were going to lose the other one. They felt enormous guilt for having ignored my symptoms for so long. I understand now that they were grieving and were unable to see the seriousness of my condition.

I had a dermoid cyst the size of a large grapefruit in my left ovary. When they removed it, they found it had seven adult teeth, as well as lots of hair inside. They also discovered I had acute appendicitis. I was lucky they discovered the cyst and stumbled upon the problems with my appendix before it burst. I was hospitalized for thirteen days and missed my third grade teacher's surprise birthday party. I was very disappointed.

After surgery, I had to find a new balance. I had to adjust to how my body felt without a giant tumor throwing me off balance. I had to adjust to the constant burning in my abdomen. My parents had to adjust to the shift in balance from having one child who had died and three healthy ones remaining, to having a child who had experienced a significant health scare that could have led to another tragedy. This fear of something bad happening to me affected my parents' ability to let go as I got older. It was especially difficult for my dad to let me go as I moved away for college and then to my first teaching job across the country in California. That is a story for later.

The Tipping Point

My self-care really began from the moment I found out I was pregnant. I knew that I had to take care of myself in order to take care of my growing baby. Luckily I craved fruit, vegetables, and milk. I could no longer drink pop as I found the taste disgusting. Even the thought of fast food such as French fries made me feel sick. I began to carry a lunch bag with fruits and veggies in it when we traveled and at work. I ate when I was hungry and I used the restroom when nature called. I no longer ignored my body and its needs as I had grown accustomed to doing as a school counselor. Before pregnancy, I would sometimes go all day without eating or using the restroom as I was too busy taking care of everybody else's needs and didn't have time to take care of my own. This little person growing inside me reminded me of the importance of taking good care of myself because he would suffer if I didn't.

Unfortunately, my self-care led to problems at work. I arrived in the mornings with a small box of cereal, went to the cafeteria and bought a small carton of milk, and went back to my desk to read my mail and eat a healthy breakfast during my planning period. The principal found the empty milk carton in my trash can and called me into her office to tell me that I couldn't eat breakfast at my desk. She didn't care that I was pregnant and needed to feed myself in order to feed my baby throughout the day. She didn't care that it was my planning period and that I wasn't eating in front of the students or my colleagues. She didn't care that the majority of teachers had open pop cans and candy bars on their desks that they ate throughout the day. How was this logical? My principal wrote me up and I realized that my job of taking care of myself and feeding my baby was much more important than any other job I would ever have.

In October of that school year, I had my first experience with hospitalization and bed rest and had to stay home from work for a few days. The principal didn't like it, but I decided that my job was to take care of myself and my unborn child. Shortly after this, I was hospitalized again and had to go on bed rest for the remainder of my pregnancy. The principal was upset and insisted I prepare materials for a substitute. I did what I could within the limits of doctor's orders then let it go so I could focus on taking care of my health and bringing my baby safely into this world. Once again, I learned that others can't dictate what is important to me and that I was not placed here to please others.

We were relieved when our son arrived just two days before his due date. The fear of losing him before his birth was gone. Our lives had shifted and there was no going back. When you bring a child into this world, it is a scary and wonderful thing! I know many parents feel strange about going into the hospital to give birth and then leaving the hospital with a newborn human being—and nobody questions if you're qualified to take this little person home with you. As everybody says, "They don't come with an instruction manual!" It is a HUGE responsibility. New parents are filled with love, excitement, apprehension and fear as well as so many other emotions! I remember feeling so much relief that he was born alive and healthy after going through bed rest, hospital visits, home health care nurses and much stress and anxiety for the last trimester of pregnancy. I was also filled with more love than I can begin to describe! Every time I held my newborn baby, my heart swelled to the point I thought it would explode!

I was also exhausted like I have never been at any other time in my life. Newborns rely on parents for absolutely everything so there is no time to focus on yourself in those first few weeks. It is a feat to get hit and miss sleep, especially when you are nursing! This is the downside to being the mom— nobody can breast feed for you, so you must wake up every couple of hours to feed the baby. This taught me a valuable lesson; it isn't all about you, anymore. When an infant needs you, it is difficult to find balance. I had to find a new balance.

My new balance was focused on my baby as the center of my world and all my decision-making. I actually felt great joy in this and was glad to focus on this new person in my life.

Then I had to face the issue of going back to work. Although I had told my principal from the day she hired me that I wanted to work part time, she insisted I take the full-time position and that we would work out the details for part-time after the baby arrived. I continued to ask her for a statement in writing which she continued to postpone, telling me, "Oh, it won't be a problem. You can work part-time after the birth." After all I'd gone through and after missing half of the school year, she insisted that I return to work full time. I had no choice as I had a contract to fulfill. This caused me extreme stress as I didn't want to leave this precious baby that I had devoted my life to bringing safely into this world. Thankfully, my mother and mother-in-law were willing to take turns coming to stay with us and care for him these last weeks of school. I was grateful to them as I didn't have to worry about putting him in the care of a stranger. I was continuing to learn my lessons, especially that others won't put my needs first and it is up to me to do it!

With this in mind, I told the school system that I wanted to work half-time the following year so I could spend time with my new baby. The administration sent me to another school with a different principal who gave me half-time in the middle of the day, with lunch duty as the focus of my job! Good luck finding a substitute if the baby gets sick. No substitute wants those hours when they could either take a full-time sub job or two half-day sub jobs. This also meant that my schedule was a nightmare! I had to get my baby to the sitter who lived several miles west of my home, then eat my packed lunch in the van while I drove to the school that was south and east of my home. My work hours were supposed to end thirty to forty minutes before the school day ended, but I rarely got to leave on time as there were teachers' meetings that I was expected to attend after school. Translation? I was working full-time for part-time pay and missing out on the time I so desperately wanted with my baby!

I finally got so fed up with all of the nonsense. I actually quit my job one month before my contract ended at the end of the school year. I had planned to work in the school system until my son was ten, but decided that nobody was going to take away any more of my time with my son! I was tired of others dictating what they thought should be important to me. I was taking back control of my life and getting it back in balance – a balance that felt right to me! There was no going back. I left the school system and began working as a clinical counselor.

Parenting has taught me lessons that I never would have learned otherwise. My son gave me a reason to take better care of myself and to spend less time focusing on my work and career life.

Taking (Back) Control

After leaving the security of a steady paycheck in the school system, I worked for two employers to get my feet wet, but after I had to sue the first employer just to get paid, I learned that I wanted to have more control over my career and my income. I went into private practice and have no regrets!

Private practice has brought me a level of freedom and flexibility that I would never have had working for somebody else. It has allowed me to change my schedule around my son's school schedule and activities. I was able to volunteer at his schools, attend all of his cross country and track meets, field trips, concerts, plays, speech meets, piano lessons, violin lessons, band contests, etc. It gave me the freedom to be the mom, a once-in-a-lifetime opportunity I will treasure! It gave me a new balance, but I learned that when you work for yourself, part-time is only on paper. It requires fitting in the work around the other priorities in your life. I found myself working at night and on weekends to keep up with the bookkeeping, phone calls, scheduling, report-writing, etc. so I could have the benefit of flexibility. In my life, it has all been worth it as I feel like I have been able to have the best of both worlds—career and parenthood.

As my son got older and busier with activities, my life balance shifted and I didn't have much time for myself. I was running back and forth between my two full-time jobs—working and parenting—and had no time left for me. His high school years left me exhausted, especially his senior year. My husband and I are still recovering! I gained weight, was hit and miss at the gym, didn't do any scrapbooking in my scrapbooking room for three years, and allowed the clutter to creep into our home. I didn't read books that I bought, I neglected friendships, I postponed work projects (including finishing this book), and I neglected fun activities that I used to enjoy. So I went on a mission to take back my life and to find my new balance!

Since my son graduated, my husband, Quinn, and I have enjoyed <u>not</u> living at the school and <u>not</u> having to constantly rearrange our work schedules around his ever-changing activity schedule. I have made it to the gym more often instead of just donating our monthly membership fee. I have scheduled time with friends and have called them occasionally. I have cleaned out the clutter in the office, storage room and scrapbooking room so I can start working on my projects again. I have focused on getting more sleep, eating healthier and losing weight so I can feel more like myself again. I started a book club/coaching group at my office and bought audio books as well as other books at the local library book sale. I cook using home-grown veggies from our garden and we eat apples from our trees instead of eating out frequently as we did before—because we were constantly on the run. I bought a few scrapbooking supplies in preparation for actually using them! My husband and I began dating again. We occasionally eat at a restaurant, go to concerts, walk in the evenings, play pool downstairs, and we have even gone to a few movies in theatres! It had been so long since we had gone to a movie in a theatre that we had to figure out the whole new system—ordering tickets online, using a Kiosk at the theatre, and sitting in their new comfy reclining chairs. Wow! Who knew? I am excited to find this new balance!!

Finding balance at each new stage of life is an ongoing journey. When my son began college, I felt like I was taking back control of my schedule, my eating habits, my bedtime, my exercise, my work and my fun. Raising a child has been a wonderful and challenging experience, one that I am grateful to have had and that I wouldn't trade for anything else in the world. Our son is an amazing human being and I feel privileged to have had the opportunity to be his mom. That being said, I am excited about the prospect of getting back to doing the things I put on hold over the past twenty years and to focus on my life in a different way. Parenting is a full-time job with no vacation days!

I can see how the balance in my life has shifted repeatedly with job changes and my son's fluctuating schedule. Balance is not stagnant and is not set in stone. It is flowing like a river. You must learn to navigate the sandbars, the trees, the twists and turns, the islands, the currents, the rapids and the rocks. You must work to stay balanced and not tip the canoe as you meet these obstacles. If you don't look ahead, you may not see the obstacles coming your way and overcorrect. If you shift the balance too far, you'll spill into the depths then have to work hard just to keep your head above water so you don't drown. Or you'll get so battered that you can't upright your canoe and climb back in, regain your balance and get it back on course. You must learn how to use your paddles to steer, how to adjust for the obstacles, and how to regulate your speed as you navigate and find your balance.

Get Ready!

There will be times in your life when you'll run up against different obstacles, so be prepared to learn a new way to get back in balance. When you successfully navigate around an island, you learn some skills, but they aren't necessarily the same skills you'll need to navigate the rapids. Adjusting, keeping your eyes on the goal, recognizing obstacles and having a partner or two to help navigate will help you to maintain balance, even in difficult circumstances.

I hope you will climb aboard with confidence as I help you to navigate the journey of finding and maintaining your life balance. To get the most out of this book, get a pen or pencil, find a comfortable place to read and write, grab a notebook or a journal and let's get started!

The book is laid out to cover ten areas of life with ideas for creating balance in each area. We will begin with a self-evaluation of values and prioritizing time to determine which areas need the most attention. I will ask you to make a commitment to yourself. Then we will begin covering Self-Care, Relationships, Your Environment, Work/Career, Finances, Education, Spiritual Well-Being, Community,

Fun/Creativity, and Finding Meaning and Purpose. There are exercises in each chapter to help you focus on your life, the obstacles you may be experiencing, and the steps you may take to overcome those obstacles and create more balance. I am confident that if you read and do the exercises, you will find some strategies and tools that will help you to feel more balanced. It is time to stop spinning and begin living a more balanced life!

Chapter 2: Assessing Your Balance

"It's all about quality of life and finding a happy balance between work and friends and family."
—Philip Green

How many times have you felt your life is off-kilter, off-center, not aligning with who you are or what you feel is important? You may not be able to name it, but you realize that something isn't quite right. You know you aren't at your best and may have difficulty figuring out what is wrong. If you look carefully at what is most important to you, you may realize that how you are living your life doesn't match with what you believe your priorities are. In short, your life has become out of balance. Balancing your life is like eating a well-balanced meal. You need a little bit of a variety to maintain health and well-being. Too much or too little in any of the food groups can throw your body out of balance. The same is true in balancing the areas of your life. For example, too much work and not enough self-care can lead to physical and emotional health issues.

Balance is all about managing time efficiently to incorporate what's most important. If you don't schedule in all aspects of your life, there will be imbalance.

What exactly is balance? Webster's Dictionary defines balance as "mental and emotional steadiness," or "to bring into harmony or proportion," or "an aesthetically pleasing integration of elements." When you are living a balanced life, you experience "mental and emotional steadiness." You know your life is working, like a well-oiled machine. You don't experience extreme ups and downs but smaller peaks and valleys, a smoother ride. When living a balanced life, you also experience "harmony and proportion" instead of cacophony or dissonance. When you are in harmony with your true self, you are at peace. As for the third meaning, when your life is in balance it becomes "an aesthetically pleasing integration of elements." If you think of all the areas of your life as elements, you are trying to integrate those elements so your life becomes a pleasing portrait of who you are. You create a life that is like a beautiful work of art.

Some people wonder if there is such a thing as a balanced life. I am here to tell you there is! Each of us is responsible for creating our own balanced life and I am here to help you. There are no magic pills, no magic words, but each of us holds the key to creating our balanced life in a formula that we create and put into action. It won't look like anybody else's formula, but it will be one that works for you.

Let's begin with an exercise to help you think about your life and where you feel you are as far as balance. I'd like you to find a tool of your preference to record your thoughts and feelings as you do the exercises throughout this book. You may choose a notebook, journal, computer, audio recorder, or any other device that works for you. You may want to make it portable so you can take it with you and record thoughts or feelings as they arise throughout the day. The easier it is to access, the more useful it will be. It's not enough to just think about the questions. Recording your answers will help you to learn and grow more quickly than thinking about your answers. You have to use a different part of your brain to write than you do to think which helps your brain to sort out information in a more objective manner than thinking alone. Trust me on this. In my experience as a professional counselor, I have found clients who write grow much quicker than those who don't.

Throughout this book I've provided exercises to help you work through the concepts. I will describe the exercise then provide an example and space for your own work. Let's get started.

EXERCISE 1: Think of the various areas that make up your life and write them down in a column, or use the columns I've provided on the worksheet that follows. Most people think of areas such as: health or self-care, family, friends, work, finances, spirituality (or personal growth or religion), fun, education, community and personal environment. You may have some other categories to add or may prefer to label your categories in a way that is more meaningful to you. As long as it makes sense to you, it doesn't matter to me. This is a process in which you are the teacher for yourself as well as the student, so you can choose what fits best with your style and is going to help you learn the most. I am here to coach and support you.

After creating your categories, create three columns next to them. In the first column, number your categories **in order of importance** to you, with the number "1" being your first priority, etc.

In the next column, number your categories in the order in which you currently (or usually) **spend the most time.**

Now, beneath the columns, write down your thoughts about how your priorities match up with your time spent on them. Do they match evenly? Is your number one priority the area in which you spend most of your time? Is there an area that needs your attention? Is there more than one area that needs your attention? Do you feel like your life is in pretty good balance for you? You may use the space at the end of the exercise to answer these questions before moving on to Column 3.

Finally, in the third column, number your areas in the order in which they **need your greatest attention** in order to create a more balanced life. For example, if your health is important to you, but has suffered because you have spent most of your time working, you may put a number 1 in the third column next to health to show that it is the first area you want to carve out some time to improve. The things you already feel you are doing well move to a lower priority in the third column because they don't need as much immediate attention.

Your paper may look something like this:

Self-Assessment

	Order of Importance	How I Spend My Time	Needs Most Attention
Self Care/ Health	2	5	1
Family	1	3	2
Friends/Social	6	7	5
Work	7	1	6
Finances	4	8	4
Spirituality	5	9	7
Fun	8	10	8
Education	9	4	9
Environment/ Surroundings	10	6	10
Community	11	2	11
Purpose/Meaning	3	11	3

Now you try it. Here is the blank table for you to fill in.

Self-Assessment

	Order of Importance	How I Spend My Time	Needs Most Attention
Self Care/ Health			
Family			
Friends/Social			
Work			
Finances			
Spirituality			
Fun			
Education			
Environment/ Surroundings			
Community			
Purpose/Meaning			

After completing the first two columns, write your thoughts about how your priorities match up with your time spent on them. Is your number one priority the area in which you spend most of your time? Is there an area that needs your attention? Is there more than one area that needs your attention? Do you feel like your life is in pretty good balance for you?

_____

_____

_____

_____

_____

_____

_____

_____

_____

Keep this assessment handy as you will be using it throughout this book. Remember this exercise is just an example. You may make any changes or adjustments that are useful to you. You may even choose to use some numbers more than once. For example, if something is extremely low on your priority list you may label it 10 and may find something else that is also low on your list so may also label it 10. If you are currently spending approximately the same amount of time in more than one area, you may use the same number for all of those areas. The third column, however, I'd like you to label in order of importance to you to focus your attention. If you label four things as number 1, it will be more difficult to focus your energy and make improvements quickly. We will address them all. You just need to choose a starting point.

If the table is not your preference, a pie chart is another example of how you can chart the way you are currently spending your time. Make a pie chart with the areas of your life as you see them. Determine how much time you are currently spending in each area. Then make another pie chart to show the amount of time you would like to be spending in each area. Obviously, your chart won't be equally divided because getting your life in balance doesn't require the exact same amount of time in each area. You determine what amount of time you need to spend in each area to feel healthy and in balance. Once again, keep this handy as you will be referring back to it and may need to make adjustments.

EXERCISE 2: You will find a Time Management Chart to follow and in Appendix A at the back of this book. You may copy it and fill it in or use it as an example as you create your own. Fill out the chart as completely as you can this week to measure where you are currently spending your time. You may think you know where your time is being spent, but you may be surprised at how much of it is not accounted for or is being spent mindlessly in areas of your life that are low on your priority list. You may use highlighters in various colors to signify the various areas of your life or you may create a key of symbols to use as shortcuts. You may want to break down the time blocks into 15-minute increments. The point of this exercise is to see where your time is currently being spent. You will want to use this as a tool to fine tune your balance as you go through this book. You will be amazed at how it changes as you take back control of your time to align it with the things that mean the most to you!

Time Management Chart			
Time	Sunday	Monday	Tuesday
6-7 a.m.			
7-8 a.m.			
8-9 a.m.			
9-10 a.m.			
10-11 a.m.			
11 a.m.- 12 p.m.			
12-1 p.m.			
1-2 p.m.			
2-3 p.m.			
3-4 p.m.			
4-5 p.m.			
5-6 p.m.			
6-7 p.m.			
7-8 p.m.			
8-9 p.m.			
9-10 p.m.			
10-11 p.m.			
11 p.m.– 12 a.m.			

Time Management Chart			
Wednesday	Thursday	Friday	Saturday

Chapter 3: Getting Started

"The way to get started is to quit talking and begin doing."
—*Walt Disney*

Now that you have decided on the areas of your life that you want to improve, it is time to get started! For many people, the most difficult part of accomplishing any goal is getting started. I hear this from clients over and over again, "I have so much to do, and I don't know where to begin!" Or they say, "I know I need to do . . ., but I just don't know how to get started!" Some clients are paralyzed with the fear of doing it wrong so they never initiate action. If any of these comments sound familiar to you, help has arrived.

Know up front, there is no right or wrong place to begin. The most important thing is that you <u>do</u> begin! Most people use Exercise 1 to identify a good starting point. They tend to go with the area in column 3 they labeled as needing the most attention. Others choose an area that is more pressing and causing them stress, that they need to resolve before they can focus on the area where they really want to devote their energy. Once they resolve the more urgent issue, they feel free and can give their full attention to what is most important to them.

You have the freedom to choose what works best for you. You may choose to read this book in the order in which I created it, or you may decide to first target the area you need to concentrate on most. No matter how you prefer to do it, realize <u>all areas</u> will be addressed and each of them will get the consideration they deserve.

Commitment

"The secret of change is to focus all of your energy, not on fighting the old, but on building the new."
—Socrates (a fictional character from Dan Millman's book, Way of the Peaceful Warrior)

The main thing necessary for success is Commitment. When you have decided to start, commit to whatever it is you want to do. No plan will work without a strong commitment to it!

Ask yourself these questions:

1. How important is this for me to accomplish?
2. How will I feel when I accomplish this goal?
3. How will I feel if I don't accomplish this goal?
4. How will my life improve as a result of achieving this goal?

Have you ever looked back at goals that have remained on your to do list for ages? Have you thought about what has prevented you from reaching those goals? For some people it is fear.

It may be <u>fear of failure</u>. The thought process may sound like this: "What if I try and fail? What will people think? That's a lot of work to do and it would all be wasted if I failed. I may have to start all over! What if I keep trying and never accomplish it? People will think I'm a loser. It's just easier not to start."

It may be <u>fear of success</u>. "What happens if I succeed? What will I do with the time I usually spend thinking, worrying, procrastinating about this? What will people think of me if I actually do it? Will they expect more of me? If I accomplish this goal, I won't have any excuses. People will see I'm more capable than I've been letting on! This means more work! I won't be able to slack off any more! I don't know if I want to have the bar raised. I've had it pretty good sitting back and not putting forth the effort. I'm not really getting the life I want, but it's okay. It's easier than working hard."

For some, the obstacle is <u>uncertainty</u>. "What will happen if I accomplish this goal? Will it change my life? Will I be able to deal with all the changes that accompany reaching this goal? Do I really want this? What if I get there and realize this isn't really the goal I wanted? What if I get there and realize that I was happier before I attempted this goal? Will I lose relationships as a result? Will I have to move? I'm not sure that I want to deal with all of these unknowns, so maybe I'll just put it on the back burner, again."

Doubt is the obstacle for others. "I don't know why I think I can do this. Nobody else thinks I can. I've tried and failed to meet similar goals in the past. This will probably turn out like those did. Maybe I'll think about it later, when I'm at a better place in my life. This is probably not the right/best time for me to be trying something new."

Having no plan in mind holds some people back. They may have a desire, but haven't thought at all about how they may put it in motion. A goal without a plan to reach it will fail.

The inability to see the end objective may get in the way for others. Why do you want to achieve this goal? What will you be, do, or have as a result of accomplishing this goal? How will accomplishing this goal improve or enhance your life?

Now that you've faced some of the obstacles, it's time to decide how to get started. The first step is to choose a direction. You have ideas from the earlier exercises. Choose a direction that looks appealing to you. This is not a life or death decision. If you start down a path and realize you are going the wrong direction, you can always stop, go back to the intersection and choose a new path. For every goal you have, there are many roads you can take to get there. Just because one path doesn't feel right doesn't mean you have to give up the goal. The most important thing is that you choose a path and commit to moving toward your goal.

Once you have chosen a direction, the next big question is: how will you stay committed to the journey, and what is your plan for follow through? This is where a contract that shows your commitment to the goal can be helpful. There is power to committing to things in writing. When you sign a contract, even with yourself, you tend to take it more seriously.

So let's create a contract. I've included an example. Start by stating your goal in the positive present tense such as, "I complete the rough draft of my book and will turn it over to the editors by December 31, 2018." When you state it this way instead of "I will _____" or "I am going to _____", you are already tapping into the part of your brain that takes action. It isn't something that you will eventually get around to doing, but it's being done right now! This shows your commitment, causes you to feel the shift, and gain confidence that it will be done by the deadline. Be very clear and specific while making sure that the goal you are setting is achievable. Imagine yourself having already reached your goal so you really feel what it will be like. Decide that nothing will stop you from reaching it. Commit to making a plan to deal with all possible obstacles and know that your determination and commitment will make your dream a reality.

Choose a start date and commit to it. Also choose an end date so you can begin with the end in mind. Deadlines are essential to accomplishing goals. When you can see that there is light at the end of the tunnel, you know the journey is doable. Would you start a race if you didn't know how far it was to the finish line? Too often, people choose a start date, but neglect to set an end date, thereby leaving themselves the wiggle room to only half-heartedly commit to the project.

Use an accountability partner. This is someone you trust to hold you to your promise to yourself to reach this goal. It may be a friend, spouse, coworker, family member, life coach, etc. Set regular dates with this person to share the successes and obstacles on your path to your goals. Make sure this person won't let you off the hook. That won't help you to reach your goal by your deadline.

Reward yourself for each small success, building up to larger rewards for achieving bigger goals. Rewards don't need to cost any money. They can involve the gift of time for yourself to do something that energizes you or brings you joy. When you reach the final goal on that path, you must CELEBRATE! This is NOT negotiable! You decide the celebration. This is your largest reward and will help you to mark the success! This also sets you up for the mindset of reaching another goal to earn another celebration!

EXERCISE 1: Make a contract with yourself. It should look something like this:

I, _____, am committing myself to the follow-through and completion of the following goal:

Beginning on (date) _____, I (What are you going to do? Be specific.)

_____

_____

_____

_____by

(completion date) _____

I will ask _____ to be my accountability partner to hold me to the follow-through and completion of this goal. We will meet (how often, how long and where?) _____

_____

_____

_____I will reward myself for completing small steps with _____

_____

_____

Upon completion of this goal, I will celebrate by _____

_____

_____

Signed by _____

Date_____

Accountability Partner(s) Signature(s) _____

_____

Date _____

Accountability Partner(s) Signature(s) _____

_____

Date _____

EXERCISE 2: Choose a direction, a goal, a starting place. What do you really want in your life? What is the smallest step you could take to move down the path toward that goal?

_____

_____

_____

_____

_____

_____

How will you feel when you have taken the first step?

_____

_____

_____

How will you feel when you reach your goal?

_____

_____

_____

On a scale of 1-10, how committed are you to this goal? _____

What are you willing to do to show your commitment to this goal? How will you remind yourself on a daily basis of this commitment?

_____

_____

_____

_____

_____

Congratulations! You are ready to take action. Making a commitment to yourself is the beginning of creating the balance you want in your life.

Chapter 4: Learning Self-Care

*"If you think selfish is a dirty word, learn to practice
extreme self-care – put yourself at the top of the list and
everyone else will benefit!"*
—*Cheryl Richardson*

No matter where clients choose to direct their attention, it seems that what often causes them stress is neglect of self-care. Once we concentrate on setting aside some time for self-care, much stress is relieved and clients can gain energy to tackle the other areas of their lives.

Take the example of Melanie, a lovely 29-year-old married mother of two beautiful young children. She was working on a home business in sales and was frustrated because she was unable to grow her business and accomplish all that she wanted to accomplish. She was exhausted, drowning in stress and her physical health was taking a beating. She had been sick for two weeks and couldn't seem to kick it. She hired me to coach her on her business and I immediately assigned her homework related to her self-care.

She had to start with getting enough sleep every day, ideally she'd go to bed at the same time every night and get up at the same time every morning. After we established this sleep routine, we focused on eating meals at regular intervals. She worked on eating healthy foods instead of fast food and she carved out time to eat. The next step was to establish a little bit of time for herself every day, even if it was only fifteen minutes. Thirty to sixty minutes would be better, but it's better to start with something that is easily attainable and gradually increase the time. Then Melanie had to agree to take time to do something she enjoyed, and this did not

24

include time with her children, family or work. I assigned her two exercises, morning pages and a weekly artist's date, taken from *The Artist's Way* by Julie Cameron. We'll talk more about these practices in the spirituality section, but I'll give you a brief description of the exercises here. The morning pages are three handwritten pages of stream of consciousness writing done at the start of each day. The artist's date is a block of time set aside to nurture your creative consciousness by yourself. It's a play date with you!

Melanie took her first artist's date to an art gallery in Omaha that she hadn't visited in a long time. She came back refreshed. After some self-care, she was ready to work on other things, such as her business. As she began feeling better, recovering her health and regaining energy and motivation, we discussed the changes and how they occurred. She told me that she thought I was crazy when we I insisted we start with self-care rather than her pressing business issues. She didn't see the connection until she did the homework, made the changes, and noticed immediate relief. She apologized for doubting me. Can you relate to Melanie's story? It is easy to lose sight of how important self-care is to balancing your life until you are falling down.

Time for Self

"Saying no can be the ultimate self-care."
—*Claudia Black*

When was the last time you spent an hour with yourself, just being, relaxing, loving yourself? Most people say, "I couldn't spend an hour with myself! I'm too busy! My family needs me, I have work that needs to be done, my house is a mess and I need to go to the grocery store so I can cook dinner! When do I have time to spend an hour doing something I want to do?" The problem with not taking time for yourself is that you run yourself down and you have nothing left to give to all the people and other activities in your life that you say are so important.

Creativity is essential to me in my self-care. When I don't get to be creative for a while, I get crabby, I feel stressed and I am not much fun. When my son was in elementary school and I was stressed from trying to balance work, parenting, marriage, home demands, etc., I had to retreat to my scrapbooking room on a Saturday or Sunday and allow my husband to be the parent in charge so I could have some creative time to unwind and to get in touch with myself and my creativity. I could tell when I had been deprived of this time for too long because my husband would suggest that he take my son somewhere for an activity so I could work in my scrapbooking room. He knew that I would be much more pleasant and relaxed after having several hours to myself to be creative without interruption or demands on my time.

Have you ever been driving and realized your gas tank was nearly empty? Did you take time out to fill it, or did you keep your fingers crossed and continue driving until it ran out of gas? What was the result? Did you make it to your destination or not? Were you late? Did you miss whatever you thought was so important? Or did you decide that it was more important to fill up rather than push it? Did you slow down, and pull off the road for a few minutes to refuel, or did you continue to race along in the fast lane knowing that you could come to a complete stop at any moment?

It's a no-brainer to realize that you need to fill a vehicle with gas **before** it becomes completely empty or you'll be in trouble and risk causing damage to your means of transportation. If it's bad enough, you may temporarily **lose** that transportation and have to find another way to get around, which is not only inconvenient, but costly! The same is true if you don't take the time to refuel yourself. Are you willing to take a chance, cross your fingers, and hope you can get there, but unwilling to slow down, refuel, and make sure you do get there?

Often people take better care of their vehicles than they do of themselves. Car owners realize that maintenance is key to extending the life of a vehicle so they routinely check the oil, water, tires, windshield wipers, battery, air conditioning, wiper fluid, etc. How many of those same people routinely ignore their own maintenance? They don't get enough sleep. They eat fast food, fatty food, sugary food, junk food and too much food. They neglect their bodies through inactivity which has the same negative effect as driving a vehicle with no care or attention. Eventually it just won't start.

Recently I had been running errands and grocery shopping for several hours. When I got home and pulled into the garage, I turned off the vehicle and was preparing to get out and unload when I realized that I hadn't written down my mileage. I put the key back in the ignition and turned it just enough so I could see the mileage. I didn't have a reason to leave the house the remainder of the weekend. One and a half days later, as I was preparing for work the next day, I couldn't find my van keys. They weren't in their usual place. After I had emptied my purse for the third time and rechecked all the pockets, I had to accept that they were lost. As I thought back to the last time I'd used them, I decided it was worth a trip to the garage to check. When I opened the van door, the interior lights didn't come on. I had left the keys in the ignition to drain the battery for nearly two days! I knew that if I didn't take care of recharging the battery immediately, I wouldn't be able to make it to work on time the next morning. My husband got out of bed, hooked up the battery charger and found the charge was down to less than four percent! If it had drained completely, the chances of starting the van without a new battery were slim. Thankfully, we were able to recharge the battery and get the van started. But what a lesson I learned! When life is too busy and you are running on empty batteries, you need to take time to recharge or you aren't going anywhere!

Many car owners are good at keeping their vehicles spotless on the inside as well as the outside. I have a neighbor who thoroughly cleans both vehicles every weekend and they sparkle! How many of you can say you spend the time cleaning yourself up inside and out so you sparkle and shine?

Vehicle owners are usually quick to realize when there is a problem that is too large for them to handle without the professional help of a mechanic. However most people are do-it-yourselfers when it comes to self-care and don't ask for the help from which they could benefit. They refuse to go to the doctor to diagnose and take care of a health problem or even for routine maintenance such as a physical. Without the proper diagnosis and treatment, they may damage their engine or completely stop running. They could benefit from the help of a dietician to find out how best to keep the body fueled and running smoothly. They may also benefit from a personal trainer who can help with the tires and axles to keep the body moving smoothly. What about consulting with a financial advisor for financial questions? Some people could benefit from counseling to help them deal with social, emotional and mental health issues, but few have the courage to ask for such help. What about hiring a life coach for overall good health and maintenance?

I often tell clients to think of their core body as a vase or bucket that holds energy. When the bucket is full, you have plenty to give others so you pour from the top of the bucket to help fill their buckets. You pour out for your kids, your spouse or significant other, your clients, your friends and other family members, pets, volunteer work, etc. If you keep pouring, but don't stop to fill up, you'll feel empty and have nothing left to give. What makes it even worse are those people, things, circumstances, work, etc. that come along and poke holes in the bottom of your bucket to take your energy from you. These drains may come in the form of incomplete jobs around the house or at work, clutter, unhealthy relationships, vehicle or home maintenance, lack of beauty in environment, eating unhealthy food, lack of sleep or exercise, lacking personal interests or hobbies that stimulate intellect or creativity, avoiding doctor or dental care, unmet emotional or spiritual needs, work stress, work that doesn't fit with skills or abilities, inability to delegate tasks, overwhelming paperwork, inadequate finances, overspending, debt, inadequate insurance, and no plan for your financial future, to name a few. Energy drains are exactly what the name says. When you feel a loss of energy, you have just experienced an energy drain. Can you think of the last time you felt this draining sensation? Was it due to a person that you'd rather avoid because every time you are around them, you feel depleted? Was it walking into a room that needed to be cleaned or de-cluttered? Was it when you received bills at the end of the month and realized you didn't have enough money to cover them? Was it waking up in the morning still feeling tired before you even started your day? Was it when you thought about that nagging cough that should have gone away by now?

Energy Drains

"When you are feeling depreciated, angry or drained, it is a sign that other people are not open to your energy."
—*Sanaya Roman*

In her book, *Take Time for Your Life,* Cheryl Richardson addresses the need to eliminate things that drain you and replace them with things that fuel you. Energy drains are all the things (clutter, activities, relationships, or habits) that cost you energy, such as procrastinations, items on your to do list, piles of files, or any other unfinished business. As you take care of each of these items, you reclaim the energy that was attached to it, which gives you more energy to focus on what really matters to you. I have adapted Richardson's exercises in the following exercise.

EXERCISE 1: Energy drains come in many different forms. Although we have many in common, the amount of energy they deplete is different for each of us. In this exercise, I'd like you to list the things in your life that drain you. I suggest making two lists, one for drains at work, and the other for drains at home.

List your energy drains at work and at home.

Energy Drains at Work	**Energy Drains at Home**
1._____	1._____
2._____	2._____
3._____	3._____
4._____	4._____
5._____	5._____
6._____	6._____
7._____	7._____
8._____	8._____
9._____	9._____
10._____	10._____
11._____	11._____
12._____	12._____
13._____	13._____
14._____	14._____
15._____	15._____

Now look at your lists. Make a commitment to take care of all the things on your list. Keep in mind this edict: "Do it, dump it, or delegate it." You will experience great relief in "whittling down" your energy drain list which will free you up to include more things that energize you in your life.

Some things on your list will be easier to eliminate than others. For example, you can get rid of some clutter by hauling it to the trash or to a donation center. But what about people in your life that drain your energy? What if you have a coworker you must work with? Unless you change jobs, you can't eliminate your coworker completely from your life. What about a bad neighbor, or a family member who pushes your buttons or exhausts you? What do you do when you can't completely eliminate some of these people or situations?

I recommend brainstorming ideas with others who know these human energy drains. Consider the annoying coworker that you must work with daily. Is there a way to rearrange your office space to discourage contact? Maybe you could move to a different area, move the opening of your cubicle to another side, or rearrange your furniture so you face away from the offender. I had a client whose coworkers would cut through his office or stop by and interrupt him while he was working. He was lucky. He had a door that he could close. I told him to post a sign on the door telling people he was unavailable and to give them a time when they could stop back. (If you must post a note like this, using humor always helps.) This was an inconvenience for those who wanted to cut through his office, but he was able to retrain them, and, consequently, get his work done. I also told him to get the support of his boss before he implemented his plan. Who could you consult at work to help you deal with coworkers who are on your energy drain list?

What If it is a bad neighbor? This can be challenging, so consider what they are doing that is creating a problem for you. Are other neighbors having the same issues? How do they handle it? Is the offending neighbor approachable? Could you talk to him/her? Some neighbors are unaware that their behavior is negatively affecting others and are willing to cooperate. Are they breaking any laws? If so, you could turn them in to the police and either they will change the illegal behavior or they may be forced to move. If you rent, check with the landlord about any activity that is not in compliance with the lease and let them handle it. Consider your options and consult with others.

Family members are a special challenge in the energy drain department. Some family members are easier to avoid because they live far away. You can plan a strategy for rare occasions when you have to see them to reduce the amount of time you are around them. (Restrooms are a great place to go when you need some space between you and them.)

For family members that you see on a regular basis:

- Consider limiting your contact with them. Have an escape plan in place so you can leave before your energy is depleted. Plan ahead and have a good reason that you are only available for a short time.

- Set clear boundaries about hot topics and make every effort to stay positive while you are together. If you sense that the boundaries are going to be violated, remove yourself from the situation (see restroom tip).

- Go for a walk.

- Talk to somebody else.

- Go to a different room.

- Get an important message or call that you must respond to.

- Change the subject.

- Have a sudden coughing attack that requires a drink of water or moving away from the situation.

- Observe or consult with others who seem to handle these people better than you do and get tips from them.

- Set the tone beforehand by planning an activity that keeps things positive and helps to steer conversations away from danger zones.

- Different strategies work with different people so notice the ones that work with your particular family energy drain.

- Remember that this is a temporary situation and you won't have to be around this person forever.

- Smile because this tricks your brain into feeling better. I recommend the half smile to my clients because it is easier to start small. When your brain realizes you are making the effort to smile, it will cooperate with you and will release some endorphins which will continue to make you feel better. Smiling and laughter are great ways to reduce stress and tension so find something you can laugh about with the offending party. Everybody will benefit.

Energizers

"Passion is energy. Feel the power that comes from focusing on what excites you."
—Oprah Winfrey

Energizers are all the things or activities that fuel you with a charge of fun, joy, passion, peace or comfort. They may include positive daily or weekly habits such as meditation, exercise or time with friends, family, and your spouse or life partner. List those things that impact your life in a positive way. They may be activities that you do (or want to do more of), people you like to be around, or favorite aspects of your physical environment.

EXERCISE 2: List those things that give you "fuel" or energize you at work and at home.

Energizers at Work	Energizers at Home
1._____	1._____
2._____	2._____
3._____	3._____
4._____	4._____
5._____	5._____
6._____	6._____
7._____	7._____
8._____	8._____
9._____	9._____
10._____	10._____
11._____	11._____
12._____	12._____
13._____	13._____
14._____	14._____
15._____	15._____

If you are interested in reading more by Cheryl Richardson, *Life Makeovers* offers more ideas to improve your life.

Chapter 5: Becoming Healthy

*"Everything in moderation, and there's a perfect
balance in this life if we can find it."*
—Ryan Robbins

Eating Healthy

A key aspect of taking care of our physical health is eating healthy. You hear this all of the time, but do you really understand what it means? Or do you know, but choose to ignore what your body wants and make poor eating choices, anyway?

Have you ever craved something that you knew wasn't good for you? The more you tried to deny the craving, the more you thought about it. The thoughts continued to build until you reached the point where you couldn't think of anything else. It consumed your thoughts and energy until you gave in. Maybe what you craved was readily available like the leftover doughnuts on your counter or the cookies you baked for the kids. Maybe you made a trip to the store to get what you were craving. Your craving for potato chips was so strong that you bought three bags in a variety of flavors. You got home, tore open the first bag of chips and shoved one hurriedly into your mouth, only to discover that it wasn't as good as you had hoped. So you opened the second bag, grabbed a handful of chips and shoved several in your mouth at one time. Your taste buds were greeted with disappointment. You opened the third bag with much less enthusiasm, slowly pulled out one chip, took a small bite, and didn't get the flavor rush you had hoped for. You closed all three

35

bags, put them away, and looked for something else. Did you move on to sugary snacks? Or did you take some time to listen to what your body was telling you it wanted? Your body is always speaking to you. You have just become very good at ignoring it.

When I was pregnant, my body spoke to me all the time and I was forced to listen. I could no longer ignore what it craved. I had to give it what it wanted and what my baby needed. I craved milk, fruit and vegetables. I couldn't eat anything greasy, so fast food restaurants were out. No more French fries or burgers. Pop (or soda, as some people call it) tasted disgusting to me so I wasn't even tempted to have a sip of my husband's Coke. I drank milk and water. I had to eat when I was hungry and stop when I was full. When we traveled I carried an insulated lunch bag with baby carrots, celery, grapes, apples, oranges and berries. I rarely wanted anything sweet such as cookies, cake, ice cream or candy. The one sweet thing I craved was poppy seed kolaches. Never in my life had I craved kolaches, but Quinn is Czech so I figured the Czech baby I was incubating knew what he wanted. I tried various bakeries in town, but none of them had genuine kolaches like the older Czech women made where we grew up. They were all too sweet. My mother had to come and help me bake them to satisfy my craving.

Pregnancy cravings were much different than any cravings I had experienced before. These were not the conscious thoughts or desires for sweet or salty that usually accompanied distressful feelings. I wasn't seeking to mask feelings or to alleviate stress or to seek comfort. My body spoke to me and I listened. For years afterward, when old habits returned, I told people that I needed to go back to eating as I did when I was pregnant. They would laugh and make comments about the large quantities of food that some pregnant women consume. I had to explain that I did my healthiest eating when I was pregnant because I listened to my body instead of my emotions.

Have you had a similar experience when you listened to your body and chose to eat healthy? How was that different than giving in to a craving that left you disappointed? I'm not saying that you should never satisfy a craving, but ask yourself, "What is it I really want? Am I really hungry? Or am I experiencing an uncomfortable feeling that I don't want to feel?" If it is a feeling, how can you deal with the feeling in a healthy way? For example, if you are feeling stress over a work situation, is there someone you could talk to? If not, what about writing it down in a journal to sort out your feelings? Would going for a walk or listening to some relaxing music help to calm the feelings? Have you tried some yoga poses or meditation to relax? What about doing something creative – writing poetry, drawing, painting, sewing, gardening, scrapbooking or cooking? What about experiencing nature? Quite often, just getting outside, feeling the sunshine, breathing in the fresh air, looking at the trees, flowers, grass, plants, and animals can have a calming effect and remind you of your place in this world.

EXERCISE 1: Pay attention to your cravings this week. Keep a journal of what you are craving, when it occurs and how you are feeling. Do you observe any patterns? Is there a time of day you are hungrier and are more apt to make an unhealthy choice? How can you prepare yourself for this? Will you have some healthy snacks readily available? Choose your healthy snacks and keep some at home, at work and in your purse or briefcase or a snack box you can carry in your vehicle.

_____

_____

_____

_____

_____

_____

_____

_____

EXERCISE 2: As you begin paying attention to your body and what it wants, observe how you feel when you truly listen to it and feed it the nutrients it desires. Notice how your body feels when you fuel it with healthy food. Notice your energy level. Notice your ability to think and concentrate. Record your observations in your journal.

_____

_____

_____

_____

_____

_____

_____

EXERCISE 3: If you are unsure what healthy food is, do some research. Talk with your doctor or a dietitian. Create a list of healthy choices that don't cause you to feel deprived but include foods that you enjoy. Eating healthy does NOT have to consist of only lettuce and cottage cheese! If you create the right balance, you can eat whatever you want, keeping in mind the portions and frequency. If you don't think you can do this on your own, there are many businesses and support groups that will help you with this (Weight Watchers is the plan I use; Diet Center; Jenny Craig; TOPS; Overeaters Anonymous, etc.). The list is long so do your research and find a plan that fits your needs and feels like something you will be able to maintain. When you begin eating healthier and feeling better, it will have a positive impact on the rest of your life. Bon Appétit!

Benefits of Exercise

"It's about having an active lifestyle, staying healthy, and making the right decisions. Life is about balance. Not everybody wants to run a marathon, but we could all start working out and being active, whether you walk to work or take an extra flight of stairs."
—Apolo Ohno

You often hear that "your body is your temple", but what does that really mean? Do you treat your body with reverence? Do you acknowledge your higher self, God within, by taking good care of yourself? Are you a good custodian/caretaker of your temple? How do you care for this temple that houses your soul?

Your body is truly amazing and miraculous in its ability to keep you running. I am fascinated with the body's ability to fight illness and to recover when it has been injured or abused. Consider smokers who quit. Experts say that lung health begins to improve from the moment they quit smoking. Within two or three days, the body has eliminated the nicotine in most cases. Within three months, the lung's ability to inhale and exhale is greatly improved. Shortness of breath and coughing are rare after a year. The U.S. Surgeon General's report states that after ten years of being smoke-free the danger of lung cancer plunges to less than half that of a smoker. This is astounding, considering the damage that was being done daily over years of smoking.

If the body can bounce back from years of smoking, it can bounce back after years of other neglect or abuse. Have you ever discontinued an exercise program, and then started again? What happened? I can give you a personal example. Years ago, I was busy with work and raising a young child so I didn't take time to exercise. I had allowed life to get in the way of my health. I decided to go back to the recreation center and walk the track. I was so out of shape that I couldn't even make it a mile! I had to go back to a half mile to get started. This reality-check kicked me into gear and I began a regular walking regimen, working my way up to four miles! I lost weight and kept it off for years. My body forgave me for the neglect and bounced back, allowing me to have more energy, stamina, and to get back into shape so I could take better care of myself and my family. When I began, I was afraid that there was no chance I could walk the distance I wanted to walk. As long as I showed up for my body, it showed up for me.

If it has been awhile since you have treated your body to exercise, don't give up! Your body will forgive you, so you need to forgive yourself. When you start cleaning up your temple, it will shine! If you already exercise regularly, congratulations and keep up the good work! If you haven't been exercising, think of one small step you will take this week to give your body the chance to go out and play instead of being cooped up.

EXERCISE 4: Consider an activity that your body would enjoy. What is something you have done in the past that was fun and gave your body a workout, even if it was a mild workout? There are so many ideas to choose from: walking, swimming, running, biking, hiking, dancing, basketball, soccer, aerobics, yoga, etc. Choose one activity to do this week. Start small and work your way up by adding more time or distance to your chosen activity.

This week I will:

_____

_____

_____

_____

EXERCISE 5: It is easy to get in a rut. When this happens, your body is no longer challenged, and the workout doesn't have the same impact as it did when you began. Sometimes you need to change it up. Challenge yourself to try a new activity. There are many options! What about a belly dancing class? A hula hoop class? A Zumba class? Yoga? Find information on classes at a local YMCA or gym and look for something that interests you. Sign up and see what you think after you have tried it. Maybe you will find that you enjoy it and want to continue, or maybe it isn't a good fit but it was fun to try something new. Try it out and record how you feel afterwards.

_____

_____

_____

_____

_____

_____

_____

_____

_____

Health Care

The cost of health care has become a huge issue. Often, people won't go to the doctor or dentist because they don't feel like they can afford it. They allow a small problem, such as a lump, to grow until it becomes a huge problem, such as cancer, which requires a lot more time, money, pain and recovery than it would if it had been dealt with at the first sign. I understand the financial concerns as I deal with insurance companies, high deductibles, and reduction in coverage on a daily basis in my private practice. I also see the consequences of postponing health care. Although the idea of delaying the expense seems logical at the time, I have known a long list of people who, in hindsight, wouldn't have worried so much about it and would have preferred paying for a doctor's visit and a few tests up front rather than deal with the surgeries, hospitalizations, missed work and greater expenses that could have been avoided.

I don't love going to doctor appointments. I freely admit there have been times when I postponed making an appointment because I didn't think a symptom was a big deal or that it would resolve on its own. Two and a half years ago, I finally went back to the doctor for a lump on the back of my head and neck that had been growing. I noticed that it was growing, but I kept telling myself that it was my imagination or that it wasn't a big deal because the doctor had said it looked benign. By the time I went back, it had more than doubled to the size of a small chicken egg. I had conveniently dismissed symptoms such as more frequent headaches and the reduced mobility in my neck. I now faced surgery which is a problem for me as I am very sensitive to anesthesia. Even if I had gone in sooner, I may not have been able to avoid the surgery, but the lump would have been easier to remove. As it is now, I still have numbness in my head that may never go away due to the severing of nerves.

Have you ever had a minor tooth ache that you put off? What happened? Did it go away or did it develop into something that required more time, expense and recovery, such as a root canal? I had some mouth pain in college that I ignored. When I finally went to the dentist, I found that I had "acute necrotizing ulcerative gingivitis", otherwise known as "trench mouth". I thought he was teasing me and didn't realize it was a real thing. The result was irreversible gum damage that causes the roots of one of my lower teeth to be exposed. If I had gone in sooner, maybe I could have prevented the long-term damage.

I am sure you have heard or experienced similar stories. My point is that each of us needs to be more aware of our health issues and to take action before things get worse. Find a way to take better care of your body, and it will reward you with more energy and vitality and fewer aches and pains.

EXERCISE 6: In addition to exercise (or the lack thereof), are there ways that you have neglected taking care of your physical health? Do you stay up too late, drink too much caffeine, watch too much TV? Do you neglect going to the doctor for checkups or avoid the doctor when there is something you should have checked out? Do you have regular dental checkups? What have you neglected that your physical body would appreciate you paying attention to this week? Resolve to take care of it. Make a plan to change something, even if it is as minor as going to bed 30 minutes earlier, cutting back on the number of sodas or cups of coffee, or reading instead of watching TV one night a week. Make the appointment that you have been putting off. What is the one thing you will do this week to take better care of your physical health?

_____
_____
_____
_____

"The body needs its rest, and sleep is extremely important in any health regimen. There should be three main things: eating, exercise and sleep. All three together in the right balance make for a truly healthy lifestyle."
—Rohit Shetty

Chapter 6: Living in Relationship

"You don't choose your family. They are God's gift to you, as you are to them."
—Desmond Tutu

"I believe that the greatest gift you can give your family and the world is a healthy you."
—Joyce Meyer

Time with Family

How many times do we hear people say that their families are the most important things in their lives? When I am working with clients and I ask them to make a list of their values and prioritize them, (just like you did in your self-assessment in the first chapter) family shows up at or near the top of the list, usually in first or second place. As we examine how their time is spent, we often quickly discover that time spent with family does not match up with the value clients place on it. People who do this exercise are usually sad or disappointed when they look at the reality of how they spend their time. They don't want their families to be eighth or ninth on their lists, so we take some time to work on their schedules to make them align more with their values. This isn't always an easy task as it seems that urgency often takes precedence over importance. We'll talk more about the urgency and importance in our discussion on work. Are you spending time with your family members in ways that allow you to build relationships and make memories? Or is your time

43

with them spent on the run between work and other activities, taking care of the urgent instead of the important? How do you want to be spending time with your family? If you didn't have to be concerned with work, chores, and other obligations, what would you choose to do with your family?

Relationship Bank Accounts

How are you building up your "Relationship Bank Account"? The Relationship Bank Account works like a regular bank account whereby you make deposits and take out withdrawals. You build up the account by doing things that contribute to your family member's happiness. You may make daily deposits by doing fun activities together, helping them with tasks or chores or by being a good listener. You may take out some withdrawals when you are unable to accommodate their desire due to other obligations. For example, you may miss a weekend trip because you promised to help a friend pack boxes to move. Or you may get sick and need their help.

To make deposits, focus on helping others to achieve their goals and dreams, understanding what they want and being a team or partner for the mutual satisfaction of all parties. For example, Quinn has made huge deposits into the account by supporting my dreams of getting my master's degree, opening my private practice and buying/remodeling a commercial building to house my office. I make deposits into the account through helping him achieve his dreams and goals. We have purchased two ATV's for Kennedy and Quinn to enjoy. We have become football season ticket holders for the University of Nebraska Cornhuskers. Quinn takes several hunting trips every year, which I encourage him to do—because it's important to him and his happiness. He wants to buy some land for his hobbies and he wants to retire early and travel. I will do what I can to help fulfill his dreams. This is how you build up the Relationship Bank Account. You want to keep a large balance in this account in case you need to take out a withdrawal. If you haven't been contributing to it, it will be much more difficult to take out a withdrawal when you need one.

EXERCISE 1: What are you doing to contribute to the Relationship Bank Accounts in your life?

_____

_____

_____

_____

_____

_____

_____

_____

_____

_____

Are you tagging your relationships as urgent or important, or neither? What are you doing to show the value you place on these family relationships?

_____

_____

_____

_____

_____

Immediate Family

When I think of my family, the first people that come to mind are my husband and son, quickly followed by my parents, siblings, grandparents, aunts, uncles and cousins. My husband is my family of choice. We were not born family to each other, but chose to become family for each other. This is a unique relationship with a special bond that has nothing to do with blood or a connection based on DNA. This relationship requires attention and nurturing or we run the risk of losing our connection. Before we decided to grow our family beyond the two of us, it was easy to spend time together, focusing on one another, nurturing our relationship. We lived on the road together, vacationed together, went on dates to movies and restaurants, walked in our neighborhood, watched TV shows we liked, talked and listened to each other, and laughed a lot.

EXERCISE 2: How would you like to spend time with your spouse or partner? Do you feel like you get to spend the amount of time you want to with this person? What do you do when you are together? Are you having fun together, or doing chores together, managing kids' activities and surviving the busy-ness of life?

_____

_____

_____

_____

_____

_____

_____

_____

Things changed when we became parents and added our son to our family. It became less about our relationship and all about learning to be parents. Our focus was no longer on our relationship and doing things together that we enjoyed, but now was about nurturing our child and co-parenting. Time with our son was precious and taught me a lot about love. It is a different type of love from any other I have ever experienced. I had always been goal-oriented and loved to work, but after Kennedy's birth, I no longer wanted to focus my life around my work. I wanted to continue to make sure my son was nurtured and well-cared for so I wanted to work part-time. My husband was a bit concerned about the financial ramifications, but was supportive. I wanted to be with my son for every new experience from getting his first tooth to taking his first steps. I wanted to get to know this little person that God had entrusted to us and I didn't want to miss out on the whole experience. I don't recall ever hearing a parent say, "I sure wish I had spent more time working when my kids were young." I wanted to create memories to last a lifetime!

My son and I spent a lot of time together, reading stories, writing, drawing, painting, making crafts for gifts, playing in the backyard on the special swing set made by Dad, swimming in our backyard pool, playing with friends, going to the park, the zoo and the children's museum. As he got older, I took him to Nature Preschool two mornings a week to give him experience socializing in a school setting away from me, but not so much that I felt like somebody else was getting to have all the fun with him.

As Kennedy grew older and began attending school, I became the room mother for his class every year of elementary school. This gave me a chance to watch him grow and to participate in his school life, to get to know his teachers and his classmates. Being in his classroom helped to strengthen our mother-son bond. He knew I was there for him and was interested in his life. He could share things about school and I knew the kids and teachers he was talking about and could offer ideas if he needed to problem-solve. He was proud that I was there and that all the kids knew his mom—until he reached middle school, a time that most kids want their friends to think they have no parents and are raising themselves.

When middle school arrived, it was a bit of a shock to my system as they no longer asked for room parents. Although I volunteered to help in the classroom or with activities, they didn't take me up on it. I no longer knew all of my son's friends and I didn't get to know the teachers as well. I did, however, continue to carpool for other families and to help with activities.

When Kennedy reached high school, our time together became even scarcer. He became even more involved in activities, homework and spending time with friends. He also added a job to the mix. I was involved to the extent parents were allowed to be involved with activities, which meant I spent a lot of time volunteering to make and serve food, to drive kids to events and to watch and cheer on all the kids as they ran, played music, gave speeches, performed plays, received awards, etc. Our son knew that we were there to support him as his number one fans, no matter what! We had to juggle our schedules a lot to make sure we were there for him, but we did it because we are his family and we wanted to show our love and support.

Outside of school, we made a point to spend family time together. We rode bikes, went to parks, sporting events, concerts and plays, ate meals together, played games, and did chores together. We scheduled "Family Fun Night" at least once a week (especially when he was younger) to do an activity together such as going to a restaurant, playing a game or watching a movie. We made it a point to go on family vacations every year, sometimes several times a year. It became more difficult to plan around Kennedy's busy schedule as he got older, but we did it anyway. Sometimes the trips were just for a day or a long weekend, but other trips were ten to fourteen days. These are still some of the best memories we have! When my son was having a bad day, he would come home and thumb through one of our vacation books because he said it helped him to de-stress and to feel better. During his senior year of high school, I took him to Disneyworld and Universal Studios for a week because I wanted to do something special with him before he graduated and moved on to the next phase of his life. (I even took him out of school for two days to accomplish it.) We both agree that this was a good time and gave us another opportunity to bond.

EXERCISE 3: Think about your family of choice. Do you spend time with your spouse having fun and building your relationship? Do you take time for each other? Do you talk, laugh and share stories? If not, how can you fit it into your schedule? What would be the benefits of spending time with your family vs. sending them text messages? What about children? Do you spend quality time with them, getting to know them or is life too hectic and you just feel like a taxi? What do you need to take time out from in order to schedule this important time with your family? Schedule some family time this week. Talk it over with your family and decide what you want to do together. Don't let it slip away because this time is precious.

_____
_____
_____
_____
_____
_____
_____
_____
_____

Extended Family or Family of Origin

For those of you who don't have a significant other or children, your family may be your family of origin. Maybe you have siblings that you are close to or maybe you spend a lot of time with your parents or grandparents. Or maybe, you would like to spend more time with them, but have become sidetracked with work, activities or school. It is all too easy to say, "I'll get around to it someday." I can tell you from experience, you don't always get around to it before it is too late. Although we don't want to think about it, our family members aren't always going to be available when we have the time. Consider the song "Cats in the Cradle" written by Harry Chapin in 1974 which tells the story of the father not taking time off work to be with his son and as they age, the roles are reversed and the son doesn't have time for the father. It's a sad story but one that plays out frequently. If family is important to us, we can't continue to say, "We'll get together later."

EXERCISE 4: With which family members do you wish you could spend more time? What would you like to do with them? How can you fit them into your schedule? Find the time, schedule it and journal about it. This is about making memories. What can you do to make this time memorable for you and your family member(s)?

_____

_____

_____

_____

_____

_____

_____

_____

_____

_____

_____

_____

When my son was born, I gave each of his grandparents books that had room for writing on each page. These _Tell Me Your_

Memories Grandpa or Grandma books asked one question for each day of the year. They were wonderful! The problem was that the grandpas thought they would get around to it someday, but they both ran out of time. My father-in-law died in 2004 and my father died in 2007. I helped my father-in-law fill in some of his answers while he was ill and in the hospital. We both looked forward to his story-telling time and I took a notebook in with me as there was never enough room on the pages in the little book. This was a time for us to bond. I just wish we had done it earlier so we could have completed more of the book. My father had written in his up through March, but didn't get it completed. My mother-in-law has completed hers, but my mother is still working on hers. I decided that I didn't want to run the risk of her not getting it done like my dad, so I have been videotaping interviews with her while I ask her questions about her life and her memories. We may or may not get through the book, but at least we will have had some time to bond through this activity and it gives me a chance to get to know my mother as a real person in addition to being my mother. I have found that learning about the stories of my relatives has helped me to understand more about them and myself. This is something I will pass on to my son, nieces and nephews, and future grandchildren so they may know and understand more about where they come from and to learn more about themselves.

EXERCISE 5: What are the stories in your family? If you don't know them, who does? What would it take for you to schedule a time to meet with the storytellers in your family to get the stories you want to remember and to pass on? Schedule a time to talk to a storyteller in your family this week. If you can't meet with them face to face, schedule a phone call or a video call. Make a list of questions or stories that you want to cover with them. Record the stories in some way, audio, video or in writing. Get their permission to share the stories with other family members. Now you have a gift idea for the next big holiday!

_____

_____

_____

_____

_____

_____

_____

_____

_____

EXERCISE 6: Consider the last time you were together with family. Maybe it was a family reunion, a holiday, a wedding, a baby shower or a funeral. What was the tone? How did you feel? Were there family members with whom you connected and would like to continue the connection? Are there relatives you may not have the opportunity to see again due to time or distance restraints? How can you reach out to them? Create a plan to connect with at least one relative you enjoy. Plan to get together or at least to talk on the phone or via video. If you want to pick up a conversation where you left off, make a plan to do so and journal about it.

_____

_____

_____

_____

_____

_____

Investing time in healthy family relationships helps you connect to a part of yourself in a different way as well as strengthening your bonds with others. Family relationships may offer you a sense of belonging, which is what we all want in creating a balanced life.

Chapter 7: Embracing Friendship

"True friendship multiplies the good in life and divides its evils. Strive to have friends, for life without friends is like life on a desert island... to find one real friend in a lifetime is good fortune; to keep him is a blessing."
—*Baltasar Gracian*

"A friend is one that knows you as you are, understands where you have been, accepts what you have become, and still, gently allows you to grow."
—*William Shakespeare*

Whom do you consider friends? Are they the people you grew up with, work colleagues, college pals, social media connections, your spouse or significant other, or others? We use the term "friend" loosely in our culture without much thought as to what it really means. When I am working with clients and they mention friends, I ask questions so I can understand whom they consider friends and why. I've discovered that many people use the term to cover acquaintances or anybody they have a connection to in some way. As we explore the relationship, most people come to the realization that they have lots of acquaintances, but not many close friends.

Have you ever examined your relationships to determine who your true friends are? If you haven't, I recommend you explore this concept. First of all, identify the qualities you look for in a true friend. For example, most people look for someone who is trustworthy so they can share confidences without fear of them being shared with others. This is very important, especially in this age of technology where anything you say can and will be shared on social media instantaneously! A quality that I look for is kindness. If somebody doesn't treat me with kindness, why would I choose to spend my precious time with him or her? I also look for friends who treat me with respect. I care too much about myself to waste time with someone who is disrespectful of me and my feelings. I treat myself and others with respect and expect them to treat me with the same respect. People who are mean-spirited or abusive in any way are not the type of people I want in my life so I don't make space for them.

An example of a true friend from my own life is Jen. She and I grew up and attended school together from Kindergarten through 12th Grade. We went to different colleges but planned to travel the world together after graduation. Our lives took us in different directions. She moved to a different state and traveled the world with her work. I traveled some, mostly in the U.S., took a teaching job in California, did grad school, met Quinn, got married and had a child. Jen was in my wedding eight years after high school. She chose to marry and have children later than I did, so our timing was very different. Through it all, we have kept in touch. When she was single, I would drive to see her. When Quinn and I were living on the road and he accumulated frequent flyer points, I would fly to Minneapolis to spend a few days with her. She introduced me to the Harry Potter books, of which I am a big fan. We met up with another friend in San Francisco for a few days when Kennedy was 15 months old. We are planning a trip to Hawaii together. I know that no matter what happens to take us in different directions, when we talk on the phone or see each other, we will pick up where we left off. We listen to each other without judgment and offer help if asked. We respect each other and enjoy each other's company. We enjoy getting our families together, but we really enjoy our time together to talk about similar interests, books, attend plays, or have deep conversations. We have a long history and know each other's growing-up families. We share a lot of childhood memories, but we have grown and evolved. I am blessed to have such a good friend in Jen.

I am fortunate to have a number of friends in my life similar to Jen. They are people I trust and know will always be there for support and encouragement, as I will be there for them. I could share more stories about my friendships, but I want you to consider yours.

I ask you again, what are the qualities you desire in a friend? If you examine your friendships and discover that you don't really have quality friendships, what do you want that you currently don't have? Sometimes you must weed out the relationships that are unhealthy or don't contribute to your growth. This can be scary because you are used to having these people in your life. Examine your relationships and ask yourself what is in each relationship for you? How does this person support and encourage you to be your best? As long as you fill your life with unhealthy relationships, there is no room for healthy relationships to show up. You teach people how to treat you and if you allow people to treat you poorly, they will continue to do so. Do these people really have your back or will they stab you in the back if given the opportunity? Are these so-called friends, givers or takers? Do they give you what you need or do they suck you dry emotionally, financially, etc.?

I have a family member who is a recovering drug addict and alcoholic. He had a tough time with weeding out the unhealthy friendships. He was used to being around people who used him and took advantage of his kindness and desperation for friends. When he had a fresh bag of pot, his "friends" showed up out of the woodwork. Where were they when he didn't have drugs they could mooch from him? I can tell you they weren't there for him when he needed real friendship. When we discussed the idea of his attending Narcotics Anonymous, he was afraid of losing his drug friends. I told him they weren't true friends anyway and he would find real friends who supported his desire for a new and improved lifestyle through a 12-step program like NA or AA (Alcoholics Anonymous). The people he met there wouldn't sabotage his efforts, but would support and encourage him on this journey.

Once he took the leap to treat himself better and to cut out the takers in his life, he was able to change his life for the better, and he found true friends who have stuck by him for many years. Having such support helped him to realize how much he had missed out on by wasting time with people who dragged him down. When I talked to him about including his story he wanted to make it clear that he was still open to having contact with his old crowd, but they were uncomfortable being around him.

"People with the same mindset will stay around," he said. "Those who don't (have the same mindset) will move on because they are uncomfortable with somebody changing his life and being in recovery mode." He is a much happier person because he has chosen to make better choices and to surround himself with positive friends who help and encourage one another toward success and acceptance.

EXERCISE 1: It's not necessarily easy to cut out the friendships that drain you, but it is definitely worth the effort. As long as you hang on to the negative relationships in your life, you leave no room for the positive ones. Is there a friendship that you need to let go of to free yourself? If you could let it go, what or whom would you have more room for in your life? _____

_____

_____

_____

EXERCISE 2: Make a list of qualities you seek in a friendship.

_____

_____

_____

_____

_____

Make a list of people you consider "friends".

_____

_____

_____

_____

_____

As you look at your lists, ask yourself if the friends you listed have the qualities you desire. If they do, congratulations! Keep them in your life and treasure them! If there are people who don't have the qualities you desire, ask yourself why you continue to keep them in your life. What is in it for you? How do they contribute to your quality of life? If there is nothing in it that benefits you, examine whether or not you really want to put the time and effort into this relationship. If you determine that this relationship costs you more than you benefit from it, consider how you may need to end it and who will support you in your efforts to make room for more positive relationships. When ending bad relationships, it is vital that you have plenty of support from people who genuinely care about you and want the best for you. Take some time to journal how you will feel when you no longer are investing in a relationship that drains you and what type of relationships you will have room for now.

You will experience the process of grieving for a while, but I promise that if you cut out the negative relationships in your life, healthy relationships will show up! By eliminating the relationships that pull you under the water, you will free yourself to float to the surface, where you can breathe again! This will help you to create the balance necessary to climb back into your canoe, take hold of your paddles, and start steering your life back to calmer waters.

Chapter 8: Being Social

"It's all about quality of life and finding a happy balance between work and friends and family."
—Philip Green

"In Hawaii, we have something called Ho'oponopono, where people come together to resolve crises and restore peace and balance."
—Duane Chapman

Time with Others

We are relational beings. We were not created to live in isolation from others. When people are isolated from others, their mental health, as well as physical health, is affected. This is why prisoners of war are isolated. It's a form of torture. They talk to themselves, cry, think about the horrors they have experienced, scream, and beg for human contact. Their imaginations run wild and they may begin to hallucinate.

It is ironic that so many people long for connections to others, yet isolate themselves and don't take the risk to reach out to others, even those with whom they already have a relationship. I am troubled by our culture and the adverse effects that social media are having on society, especially our young people. They hold stock in the number of Facebook friends they have, but don't spend quality time with real people in real time. I find it disturbing when I see a group of young people in a restaurant, all looking at their cell phones instead of making eye contact and talking with the people who are right in front of them! It is no wonder that depression is on the rise and there is a pervasive feeling of loneliness.

Although there can be benefits to sending and receiving information through social media, there are many more benefits to spending actual time, being fully present, with other human beings. This requires making eye contact, completely focusing on one another, listening carefully, and being in the moment without distractions. This is a challenge in today's world where cell phones are constantly going off with a variety of sounds to let you know that you have a text message, an email, or a social media message that wants your immediate attention. You need time to shut down distractions and give undivided attention to people you care about. You don't know how much time you will have with your loved ones, so it is extremely important that you are fully present when you are with them. It is these moments that you will cherish for the rest of your life, not the time you spent on social media.

Are there people in your life that you haven't had contact with for a while? People that you miss? Maybe you have a former teacher or neighbor, a former work colleague, or somebody that you used to see on a regular basis due to a common interest. What would it take to reach out to them, to carve out some time from your busy life to get together? How will you feel when you see them? How will you feel if you let more time pass and something happens that precludes you from ever seeing them, again?

I had this experience a few years ago with my mother who lives in Nebraska and her oldest brother who lived in California. They had tried to get all of the siblings together in Colorado a couple of years before, but my Uncle Al was unable to make it at the last minute due to health issues. I was concerned that my mother might not get to see him again, so as his 90th birthday came nearer, I urged her to go see him. I volunteered to go with her so she wouldn't have to be stressed about traveling alone. She finally agreed, and I jumped on the chance to buy the plane tickets before she could change her mind. This was one of the best decisions we made! All of her siblings were together for the last time, as my uncle died within the year. Although they talked on the phone occasionally, there was nothing that could substitute for actually being together. I observed my aunts and uncles as they were together and noticed that they looked at one another and listened to one another. Nobody was ignoring the group to be on a cell phone. They were in the moment, enjoying one another's company and taking it all in. I took pictures and made a photo book for my mom. She was so excited to get it and share it with her friends because this allowed her to re-experience the feelings she had at this final gathering. She keeps it on the coffee table. I am grateful that I could help to create a meaningful experience for my mother and her family. I know she preferred getting together while they were all alive instead of as survivors getting together at a funeral.

Too many people wait until it's too late. How would your life be different if you enjoyed the relationships now, instead of postponing getting together because you are too busy?

EXERCISE 1: I challenge you to create more balance in your life by scheduling a time to get together with someone you care about ASAP. If you can't actually see them this week, at least call them and schedule a time to meet. If they live too far away, consider scheduling a vacation to visit them. If this isn't possible, what about setting up a time to Skype or video chat? If you or they don't own a computer, could you call them to talk? Remember to remove all distractions while talking with them. Give them your full attention and enjoy the connection. Notice how you feel before, during and after you meet or talk with them. This feeling of connection is what everybody craves. When you give somebody your full attention, it is truly a gift of presence.

Whom are you going to connect with this week? _____

_____

How are you going to connect with this person?

_____

How do you feel when you think about connecting with this person?

_____

_____

_____

_____
_____

After you meet with them, journal about it. You may use a handwritten journal or one that is written on a computer. If you don't have access to either, you may use this space to get started. Then grab a notebook or piece of paper.

_____
_____
_____
_____
_____
_____
_____

EXERCISE 2: Consider an activity that you would like to do with another person. Whom do you know that is positive, uplifting, and enjoyable that you could invite to share in this activity? Think of at least three people that you could invite. Would you like it to be a group activity or a one-on-one? If you have several people to ask, you may find at least one is available. If you look at your list and decide you would like to do something with each one of them, come up with additional ideas that you would enjoy doing with each person. Remember to tell them that you want to get together with them without distractions and ask if they are willing to try the experiment of turning off the cell phone or putting it somewhere else during your time together.

With whom would you like to do an activity in the next two weeks? List at least three people to invite.

_____
_____
_____
_____
_____

What activity/activities will you propose to do together?

_____
_____

_____

_____

_____

_____

Spending time with people you enjoy without distractions is a refreshing way to regain balance in your life.

Chapter 9: Working to Live

"But if you can create an honorable livelihood, where you take your skills and use them and you earn a living from it, it gives you a sense of freedom and allows you to balance your life the way you want."
— Anita Roddick

"When you have balance in your life, work becomes an entirely different experience. There is a passion that moves you to a whole new level of fulfillment and gratitude, and that's when you can do your best . . . for yourself and for others."
—Cara Delevingne

"Work is a four-letter word." What do you think of when you hear the word "work"? How does it make you feel? Brainstorm the words that come to mind and write them down. What do you notice? Is your list full of positive words or negative? Does the word "career" conjure up different feelings and ideas?

I find it sad that statistics show the vast majority of people worldwide are dissatisfied with their jobs. In an article in *Forbes Magazine*, "Unhappy Employees Outnumber Happy Ones by Two to One Worldwide," Susan Adams gives information from a massive report by the Gallup University. Gallup gathered information from 230,000 full-time and part-time workers in 142 countries. They found that 87% of workers worldwide "are emotionally disconnected from their workplaces and less likely to be productive." They said that "the U.S. has some of the best numbers in the world, with 30% happy in their work, 52% feeling blah and 18% who hate their jobs." I won't go into all the reasons but Gallup put together a list of twelve statements regarding employee engagement. Four of them stand out as they relate to this book and the topic of balance:

1. "At work, I have the opportunity to do what I do best every day."
2. "The mission or purpose of my company makes me feel my job is important."
3. "I have a best friend at work."
4. "This last year, I have had opportunities at work to learn and grow."

When I consider the topic of balance, especially between home and work, there are some key components that can help you to strike that balance and to feel more content. The Gallup statement about having the "opportunity to do what I do best every day" is often overlooked by employers, which causes workers to feel dissatisfied and disengaged. I can't begin to count the number of times I have worked with clients who have had this complaint. They were hired for a position they were excited about—where they excelled. When they did well in that position, they were promoted out of it to something that didn't use their strengths, and frankly, wasn't interesting to them. When employers don't use their employees' skills, strengths and interests, everybody loses in the happiness and productivity departments.

I had a client who had worked as an airplane mechanic for many years. He was so good at his job that he was given a promotion, one that his spouse urged him to accept because it offered a higher salary. He took it and became depressed as he didn't feel like he was able to use his skills and interests. He had a lot more paperwork, had to get training in project management, and felt a lot less confident in his skills and abilities. He no longer enjoyed work as he had in the past. When a mechanic position opened, I encouraged him to check it out to see if it was more in line with his strengths and if it would provide more job satisfaction. He became excited about it, talked it over with his spouse, and took the position. He immediately felt more balanced in his work and home lives because he was using his hands-on strengths at work, which reduced his stress and improved his home life. His story illustrates why it's key to know your strengths and to find a position where you can use them. So-called promotions are not necessarily going to give you any more work satisfaction (other than maybe a higher paycheck), so it is important to be true to yourself when offered a "better" position.

I have had several similar work experiences. The one that pushed me over the edge was my last position in the school system where I was hired as a social skills teacher instead of as a school counselor. I felt sorely underused. Although I enjoyed the students, I didn't get satisfaction from supervising lunch. I wanted to use my education, my skills, training, and strengths to the fullest and this position didn't meet those needs. So I quit one month before school dismissed for the summer, and I began working as a counselor in the private sector, where I could use my strengths, skills, and education.

EXERCISE 1: Write about a personal experience you have had where your strengths and skills were underutilized or not used at all. How did you feel about that position? How did you feel about your employer? What did you wish would have happened in that situation?

_____

_____

_____

_____

_____

_____

_____

_____

_____

Let's look at the second statement in the Gallup study: "The mission or purpose of my company makes me feel my job is important." Do you feel like your job is important? Do you know what your company's mission is? Do you feel like your position contributes to that mission? Many people go through life seeing their job as a paycheck instead of a purpose, but work and home life will be out of balance if your values don't align with those of your company. For example, if being conscientious about the environment and recycling is important to you, but not to your employer and you witness a lot of waste at work, you may find it difficult to work for this company. You may choose to bring it to your employer's attention and work on a solution that aligns more with your values. If the employer doesn't see the value in your suggestion, you may find it difficult to stay.

EXERCISE 2: What are your current employer's mission and values? Do they match your own? What would it take for you to find meaning or purpose in your current position?

Take some time to evaluate this.

_____

_____

_____

_____

_____

_____

The third area in the Gallup survey is: "I have a best friend at work." You may have heard about a "work spouse," which could be a best friend at work or someone you work closely with on a daily basis. Many people find at least one close friend at work, someone who is in a similar position or works in the same area. Colleagues you enjoy are extremely important to your work satisfaction and to your work balance. If you don't make connections with others at work, you will likely be unhappy and move on. Why would you want to stay in a job where you don't feel a connection to your coworkers?

EXERCISE 3: Who is your best friend at work? Do you feel connected to your co-workers? Have you ever left a job because you didn't feel connected to your colleagues? Write about it.

_____

_____

_____

_____

_____

_____

_____

_____

The fourth thing that stood out from the Gallup survey was: "This last year, I have had opportunities at work to learn and grow." Have you felt stagnant at work? Have you been in a place where day after day, it seems like the same old thing? No challenges, nothing new to learn. When boredom sets in, workers become less productive. Some employers require training, but it isn't always pertinent to everyone's position. For example, when I was a school counselor, I spent two days in math training that was required for all educators in the school district, regardless of whether or not we would use it. This can be just as frustrating as having no training at all. I much preferred training that was useful to my position.

EXERCISE 4: Have you had opportunities to learn and grow at work over the past year? Describe them.

_____

_____

_____

_____

_____

_____

Did you attend job related training in the past year? Was the training useful to you? Did it help you do your work better? How did you feel about the training? Were there other opportunities you wish your employer would have provided? Did you make suggestions to your employer about future learning opportunities? If so, what were they?

_____

_____

_____

_____

_____

_____

EXERCISE 5: If you have a vision of the perfect position for you, describe it here. What aspects are essential to your enjoyment at work?

_____

_____

_____

_____

_____

_____

_____

_____

_____

_____

_____

What about **creativity** at work? Even if you aren't an artist or musician, creativity can still be part of your work. Creativity comes in lots of sizes, shapes and colors and can be as simple as finding a new way to do something or looking at a problem in new ways. If you work on an assembly line and there is a certain way that everything must be done, you may feel like you can't be creative. But what if that isn't really the case? What if you could find a new way to accomplish the same task? Maybe it is a minor detail in the way that a tool is used or the way the line is set up. Maybe you have an idea on how to make work more fun, keeping coworkers engaged and helping everyone to be more productive. Problem solving is creative and can make the job run smoother for yourself and others.

EXERCISE 6: How can you make work more creative or fun? Look at some of the smallest things you could do. Maybe there are ideas you have about rearranging the space to be more efficient, or maybe there are steps that could be simplified to make the job easier. Think about it and come up with at least one idea. Consider proposing it to your boss.

_____

_____

_____

_____
_____
_____

Effective Planning

Many clients have come to me over the years feeling stressed because they don't feel like they **plan effectively**. This causes them to be less productive and sometimes leads to issues with their supervisors. We work on some simple strategies to help manage time and plan effectively. I recommend they follow **five steps to effective planning.**

The **first step** is to **prioritize** the tasks that need to be done. What tasks are urgent and have a looming deadline? Which tasks are important? Which ones are both important and urgent, and which ones are neither urgent nor important? Use the table in the following exercise to determine where you should be focusing your energy.

EXERCISE 7: Make a list of all the tasks that need to be done, then place them in this table according to their urgency and importance. This is an easy way to prioritize your day and to decide what really needs to be done. This also makes it easy to see which things are not important so you can delegate, dump or do them later. List your tasks to be done here:

_____
_____
_____
_____
_____
_____
_____
_____

Now place them in the grid according to their importance and urgency.

	IMPORTANT	NOT IMPORTANT
URGENT		
NOT URGENT		

Something that is often overlooked is your **energy level**. The **second step is to consider your high energy and low energy times and use them to your advantage**. Schedule the most challenging tasks during your high energy time and save the least important tasks and the ones that don't require as much effort for the low energy times. Mornings are my high energy time. The problem is that I want to do everything in the morning: exercising, writing this book, taking classes or workshops, and seeing clients. I must prioritize which of these things needs to be done the next day and work the others in around the most urgent and important. My low energy time is afternoon, around 3:00 to 5:00 p.m. I use this time to check email, do my billing, make phone calls, tidy up, and run errands. Sometimes I see clients during this time as it works with their schedules, but I prefer to see them earlier so they get the more energized me.

EXERCISE 8: Take some time to figure out your **high energy times and low energy times** and write them here. Use this information as you plan how you use your time tomorrow. If you aren't sure when you are at your best, pay attention to your energy levels over the next week and record what you learn on the calendar provided.

_____

_____

_____

_____

_____

_____

_____

_____

_____

_____

_____

The third step in effective planning is to eliminate distractions. This is difficult to do in this high tech, fast-paced world where we've been trained like Pavlov's dogs to respond to every ding or ringtone from our cell phones or computers. Carve out some time to turn off the distractions. I know this sounds radical, but phones do have an "off" button. If shutting off your phone completely sounds too stressful, at least turn off the sounds and vibrations so you can give yourself the gift of freedom from distractions for a few hours. Do you remember what that is like?

Schedule a block of time when you don't respond to calls, colleagues or emails. If you have a door, close it. Post a sign letting coworkers know when you'll be available. Schedule the time you will respond to coworkers, emails, text messages and phone calls. You will be amazed what you can accomplish if you do this. Discipline yourself to stick to this schedule. According to an article in the *New York Times*, entitled "Brain, Interrupted. Does distraction matter — do interruptions make us dumber?", every time you have to stop and start a task due to distractions, it takes 20-30 minutes to get back to where you left off. If you add this up throughout a day, you will be amazed at how much time is wasted due to distractions!

EXERCISE 9: Keeping in mind your high and low energy cycles as well as the distractions that pull you away from the work you want to complete, **make a plan for your day which blocks out high energy times for you to be productive and work without distractions**. Set aside this time daily and notice how much your stress is reduced and how much more you accomplish. Here is a calendar to get you started. Make changes to customize it for your schedule.

Time Management Chart			
Time	Sunday	Monday	Tuesday
6-7 a.m.			
7-8 a.m.			
8-9 a.m.			
9-10 a.m.			
10-11 a.m.			
11 a.m.- 12 p.m.			
12-1 p.m.			
1-2 p.m.			
2-3 p.m.			
3-4 p.m.			
4-5 p.m.			
5-6 p.m.			
6-7 p.m.			
7-8 p.m.			
8-9 p.m.			
9-10 p.m.			
10-11 p.m.			
11 p.m. – 12 a.m.			

Time Management Chart			
Wednesday	Thursday	Friday	Saturday

The fourth step to consider in planning effectively **is to set time limits**. It is too easy to get bogged down with tasks that aren't urgent or important. When you set time limits on these tasks, you will feel more in control and will save yourself time and energy for tasks that are important and urgent. As I mentioned previously in the section on eliminating distractions, instead of responding to every email as it comes in, change your settings so you don't receive notifications until you are ready to deal with the email. Then stick to a time frame that allows you to respond in a timely manner and get back to the next important item on your list. When you schedule time to respond to email or phone calls, set a timer so you don't get trapped into giving away your most valuable, productive time. I suggest checking email twice a day, once in the morning and once in the afternoon. Notice how much more you accomplish when you don't have to stop and start repeatedly.

An important part of keeping your work life balanced is to complete what you set out to do within the time frame of the work day. Leave your work at work at the end of the work day. Give yourself a true break when you leave the office so you are refreshed and ready to get back to work in the morning. When you set time limits, you are in control and you set yourself up for success!

The fifth step is to plan at the end of the work day what you want to get done the following day. By doing this, you set the ball in motion to accomplish tasks that otherwise wouldn't get done when they need to be done. I do this every night. I write my list in my planner. (Yes, I do this the old-fashioned way instead of on a computer, but you can do it in whatever way is useful to you.) I have found that I accomplish a lot more this way, than if I wait and create the list in the morning. It is easy to forget my train of thought from the day before. Make a list of the top three to five tasks that need to accomplished the next day and carve out the time to get them done. Use your table of urgent and important tasks to help you prioritize. Be sure to schedule these tasks during the time frames that best fit the energy level required. When you arrive at work in the morning, you will be amazed at how much more efficient and productive you are as a result of planning the day before!

EXERCISE 10: Try planning tomorrow's work at the end of each work day. Make this a five-day experiment. Check off each day you accomplish this, then record how you felt.

Day 1 ☐   Day 2 ☐   Day 3 ☐   Day 4 ☐   Day 5 ☐

_____

_____

_____

_____

_____

_____

_____

The only point I will make is that if you get involved in these types of activities to build business and to meet people, you may find that this is one aspect that offers more fun to your work. As Mary Poppins says, every job was a bit of fun. When you find that fun—SNAP! The job's done!

When you are having fun, your life feels more balanced.

Chapter 10: Finding Financial Balance

"See money – currency - as the flow of energy and giving that cycles between you, others and me. Now let it flow kindly, fairly and mindfully."
—Rasheed Ogunlaru

Welcome to the chapter on money. This is quite possibly the area of our lives that causes the most stress, most conflict, and most concern. Most people spend an inordinate amount of time focusing on money. Have you noticed how many times a day you think about money? What are your first thoughts? "Should I be spending this money? Do we have enough in the account? What will my partner say when they see what I have spent? What if I lose my job? How will we pay the bills? Maybe I should get a second job to cover the remodeling project. I don't think we can afford to go on vacation this year. The kids need new clothes and shoes. How much will that cost?" You can quickly find yourself in a self-talk money spiral and the theme will most likely be "Is there ever enough money?"

Growing up I often heard:

"Time is money."

"Money doesn't grow on trees."

"A penny saved is a penny earned."

There is truth in these sayings, but there is also a feeling of scarcity or fear. As a child, I remember hearing adults say that wealthy people were more concerned about money than those without much. The premise was that the more people had, the more they had to lose so they spent much of their time trying to protect their assets. This seemed to be a rationale for not trying to accumulate wealth. As an adult, I've often wondered how life in a town with a population of 830 would have been different if the common belief had been one of abundance instead of scarcity.

In my growing-up family, scarcity was the fear and the reality. My dad spent money on Winston cigarettes and Tvrsky's Strawberry Vodka which left little for food and clothing for four children. Add my sister's illness into the mix and there was even less. Gram bought back-to-school shoes, snow boots and winter coats for us. Mom bought material on clearance and made our clothes when we were young. Later, when she was working two jobs, she had another woman in town make them for us. We wore them until they were ragged and our pants were above our ankles. We were on food stamps and grew a large garden. Mom and Gram canned corn, beans, beets, pickles and anything else they grew so we had food throughout the winter months. Much of our meat came from hunting or fishing. Going out to eat was a treat and didn't occur very often.

Our house was the second oldest one in town and in need of repairs that my parents couldn't afford. The green and white checkerboard linoleum floor in the dining room was peeling up as was the speckled linoleum kitchen floor. The front porch had rotting boards. The house and window trim was peeling and needed to be painted. Mom wanted to have a nice home, but the best we could do was to keep it clean, so every Saturday we cleaned it from top to bottom, including dusting every book on every shelf of our rickety black metal bookcase. We had one bathroom for six people and we shared beds and bedrooms. When I was in junior high, we got a small window air conditioner. We fought over who got to stand in front of it when we came in after being out in the 100-degree summer heat. We couldn't afford to run it all the time, so it was only turned on in extreme cases.

My mom was the one who paid the bills and managed the checkbook. There was constant stress and anxiety about finances and how the bills were going to get paid. Gram helped Mom to pay the bills, unbeknownst to Dad. He was deep into his addictions and Mom was left to figure it out. She stashed five dollars here and there to buy us some clothes, or saved for a rare vacation like the time we went to Kansas City to Worlds of Fun and a Royals baseball game for a day. I don't know how she paid for doctor's appointments. I think most of the time we just didn't go and relied on Gram who was a registered nurse for our medical care. I didn't know that people were supposed to get their teeth cleaned regularly because the only time we went to the dentist was when we were in pain. Dad's overspending caught up with them and he was forced to sell the variety store he had bought from his parents. I don't know how they managed to avoid bankruptcy, but it was close. Dad talked about saving but I didn't see it in action. If it hadn't been for Gram saving money and leaving some inheritance, my parents wouldn't have had anything for retirement. As I look at my growing-up family and how they viewed money as a scarcity, I see how it impacted me. I was a saver from the first time I was given money for Christmas or my birthday. When I began earning babysitting money in fifth grade, I saved it in a hand-me-down wallet and hid it in my bedroom. There was no allowance. We all earned our own money. In seventh grade, I started working as a janitor at the school, sweeping floors and dumping trash after school. My brothers and I worked as janitors at the school in the summers, too. We worked from 7 a.m. to 4 p.m. with a one-hour lunch break. I saved as much as I could every summer.

I paid for my clothes, school activities and entertainment. I didn't splurge on things that I didn't think were necessary. (Once I did splurge on a pair of platform shoes for the junior high prom and quickly regretted it when they began falling apart shortly after I bought them.) I bought my own car. My dad picked out the 1973 Vega Station Wagon. I then went to the local dealership and wrote the check for $750.

To this day, I am a saver. I love seeing my account balances grow, especially my investments! As I write this, I am still the proud owner and primary driver of our 20-year old Plymouth Grand Voyager minivan! Why? Because it is a reliable vehicle, is very comfortable and I hate making car payments. I know I can't drive it forever, but I know its quirks (certain door locks don't work anymore, etc.) and I hate to let it go as long as it is running fine. We could afford a new vehicle and have even test-driven some, but I keep asking "is it necessary?" Amazing how old programming continues, even when we are aware of it!

Security is important to me and I don't want to live in a constant state of fear of not having enough money like my parents did. I learned to squirrel away money like my mom, so I have money ready for the trip to Hawaii that I'm planning to take with my friend Jen. It gives me peace of mind to know that I could go today if I wanted to, and I wouldn't have to worry about how I was going to pay for it. Although Hawaii isn't a necessity, it is a splurge that I am looking forward to. As I evaluate the ways I spend money, I see that I value experiences. I would much rather go to Hawaii or on another nice vacation than spend money on a new car. As much as I love to save and invest money, I also want to enjoy the present, which is, after all, a gift. If we save everything and don't enjoy spending some of it now on having fun, we may miss out and never get to enjoy the fruits of our labor! Quinn likes to travel, too, so we take vacations every year. We have other friends who don't enjoy traveling so they splurge on local entertainment such as concerts and sporting events. It is up to each of us to determine how to balance the spending between necessities and pleasure.

Clients often show up in my office due to financial stress. Unfortunately, if they have too much financial stress, they discontinue after working with me for only a short time. I understand this and encourage them to take care of their financial health. If they are stressed about paying me, they are not going to enjoy it and they won't get as much out of it. I want our time to be helpful, fun and productive so I want them to take care of themselves. After all, that is what I teach them. If paying for sessions with me could add to their financial stress, we sometimes schedule appointments further apart or make them shorter. I also remind them that it is a matter of priorities and that sometimes they must choose between their mental and emotional health (coming to me for coaching or counseling) and giving up something else (a bad habit such as smoking, for example). It is amazing how people can find money when there is something they really want! I have occasionally been burned by a client who claims financial hardship so they delay paying me, and later I find out they spent an exorbitant amount of money on Christmas gifts or they went on an extravagant vacation or they roll into my parking lot with a brand new vehicle. This becomes a point of discussion about values, priorities and responsibilities. We work on connecting the dots so they can see that it is this very behavior that is causing them financial stress and will continue to do so as long as they continue to spend in this way.

It is very difficult for some people to discipline themselves to spend responsibly. The examples that are set by politicians, celebrities, and our government are not the best examples to follow. Look at our national debt and the unwillingness to deal with paying it off. Many people feel entitled to have what they want whether or not they can afford it. The attitude seems to be, "Why not? The government spends when they don't have the money so why shouldn't I?" Our society is a fast food, click on a button and give-it-to-me-now society and people don't want to delay gratification. Our world has become impatient and people think that rewards should come immediately and without any effort. People don't want to exercise self-control because it isn't as much fun as getting what you want right now. There are so many problems with this attitude that it is hard to cover it in a short space, but I will do my best.

When you find yourself acting out like a child and thinking, "I don't care if I don't have the money. I want it now!!" it is time to step out of the child part of yourself and step into the grownup part of yourself. In therapy, it is called Transactional Analysis or T.A. for short. The basic theory is that we all act from one of three parts of ourselves:

1. the parent
2. the child or
3. the adult.

When you want to have a tantrum because you want something now, you are acting out of your child part. Think of children who want the candy near the checkout at the grocery store. They don't think about it and plan ahead to buy it, but it is all they can think about when they see it at eye level. This is impulse buying and businesses strategically design their checkout lanes to sell to people who are thinking short-term and want immediate gratification. It works or they wouldn't do it. Children are not known for their money smarts (remember Jack and the magic beans?), so when you get in child mode, you will not be making the best financial decisions.

The parent in these situations is the one who tries to reign in the child by telling him or her "NO! You can't have it, ever!" The problem with this is that when the prospect of all fun is taken away, the child will act out and rebel against the new rule.

The solution is to act like an adult, the part of you that is rational, reasonable and will come up with a plan to get what you want . . . later, when you have planned and saved the money. The answer is "yes" so the child doesn't have to rebel and act out. The adult is the great compromiser who can help you to achieve financial success because you won't feel deprived, but you won't be overspending to satisfy the short-term impulse of wanting to have it now.

All of this comes back around to support the idea of your values. What is it that you really want in your life? What are you willing to sacrifice, plan for, and do to get it? Look back at your assessment from the beginning of this book. What are the things in your life that are most important to you? If the way you are spending your money doesn't align with what is most important to you, you will feel depleted because overspending or spending in the areas that don't align with your values is an energy drain. You must plug the holes in your spending in order to fill yourself up with the things that you really want. Remember that nothing outside of yourself will ever fill you up, so when you are trying to fill a void by overspending, you are doing the same thing as others who try to hide from their uncomfortable feelings with other addictions such as alcohol, drugs, gambling, sex, overeating, etc. You can feel hung over from overspending just as you can from drinking too much. Think about how you have felt after shopping for something you didn't need but bought impulsively. It may have felt good in the moment, but it didn't last, especially when you put it on credit and got the bill later.

Sometimes you just need to find a substitute for what you want, until you get to a point that you decide you really want it, and you have a solid plan to get it. For example, instead of eating out six times a week, you decide to cook at home, take your lunch to work, and eat out once or twice. You can save the money you would have spent on eating out for your real goal, which may be buying your own house. Instead of paying for a gym membership, you can walk outside or in the mall. You may already have exercise equipment at home that you rarely use so you could dust it off and use it, remembering what your goal was when you spent the money on it. Instead of going out to the movies, you could rent one and watch it at home making your own popcorn. You don't have to sacrifice everything! You just have to be creative in finding ways to meet that need. This could be fun!

As much as you would like to avoid the subject of debt, like the government, it must be addressed so you can create balance in your finances. I often have clients make a list of all of their debts on one side of a page. This includes any payments such as monthly car payments, credit card debt, etc. I have them include their monthly bills such as utilities, phone, transportation, food, rent, entertainment, etc. In the last column is their monthly income. Then we do the math. If your bills add up to more than your income, you must look at what can be eliminated. Obviously I wouldn't recommend eliminating food and shelter, but you could reduce your payments by shopping around for a smaller home or apartment or by reducing your restaurant visits. This exercise is usually a big wake-up call for over spenders who see it on paper and realize where their money is going. My son recently had an "aha moment" when he was cleaning his bedroom and found several restaurant receipts. He was surprised at how often he had been eating out. I encouraged him to add them up and get an idea of how much he was spending to eat out, but he was so shocked that he said he didn't want to know.

EXERCISE 1: Get out a notebook or a sheet of paper and divide it into three columns. Label the first column "Monthly Bills", label the second column "Long-term Debt" and label the third column "Monthly Income." Fill it in as I explained. Then add the totals for each column. What do you see?

Monthly Bills	Long Term Debt	Monthly Income

If you make more than your monthly bills, congratulations! You may not have to make very many changes to balance your finances. If you realize that your bills and long-term debt are greater than your income, you have some work to do.

The first step is to be honest with yourself about where you stand with your finances. As Dr. Phil McGraw says, "You can't change what you don't acknowledge." Give yourself permission to feel sad, angry, or disappointed about your situation for no more than ten minutes. Set a timer. Continuing to focus on the negative emotions will not help you to do what you need to do, but it can offer a push to get you to take action.

Next, look at your list. Are there any monthly bills that you could reduce? How? Could you change your television and internet service? Could you reduce your phone service? What about setting your thermostat a little higher in the summer and a little lower in the winter to cut back on high utility bills? Could you carpool, walk or use public transportation? (Look at the questions that follow in Exercise 3 for more ideas.)

Thirdly, look at the column with your long-term debt. Do you have a plan to pay it off? Have you ever figured out how long it will take you to pay off credit card debt if you only make the minimum monthly payments? It is quite frightening when you realize how much interest you are paying to buy that big screen TV that was on sale and you couldn't pass it up! You will soon realize that you are paying for it many times over instead of getting that great sale price! It is time to exercise self-discipline and stop buying things with a credit card unless you can pay it off every month.

Once you stop the bleeding (spending), you make a plan to increase your monthly payments. Figure out how much extra you can pay each month and begin with the highest interest rate card first. When you get that paid off, pay extra on the second highest rate card. Continue this until you've paid off all of your credit card debt. Make a commitment to yourself to only use a credit card if you have money in your bank account to cover it that day. Think of it as cash. If you are using a credit card, is it because you want the item and don't have the money and you don't want to wait until you do? Or are you using the credit card to build your credit rating by paying it off every month? If it is the latter, and you will not carry the debt over another month, then you may have the self-discipline it takes to use a credit card responsibly. If you think you will be too tempted to overspend, I encourage you to stay clear of the credit cards and stash your cash in envelopes for the things you really want. You will feel much more in control of your life and you won't carry the burden of debt.

Balancing your finances can offer you freedom and peace of mind. Consider your values and goals so you create a financial plan that feels great—one that you are excited about and that will improve your life, offering you more of what you want and less of what you don't want. It is more than just spending less and making more. When you align your finances with your values, your life becomes easier, you are happier and there is less struggle.

EXERCISE 2: Consider your own views on money.

1. Do you spend more than you make? How often? How do you feel about it?

    _____

    _____

    _____

    _____

    _____

2. Do you waste money on things that are unnecessary or don't give you great pleasure? Identify these things.

    _____

    _____

    _____

    _____

    _____

3. Do you not spend enough in the areas that count (such as self-care: dental care, doctor appointments, prescriptions, healthy food, vision and hearing care, etc.)? In which areas should you be spending but aren't?

    _____

    _____

    _____

    _____

    _____

4. Do you stick to a budget? If not, why not? Be honest with yourself about this.

    _____

    _____

    _____

    _____

    _____

5. Do you and your significant other argue or disagree about money? How often? How is it resolved or is it ongoing?

_____

_____

_____

_____

_____

_____

6. Do you save for the future? How much? Are you taking advantage of your employer's retirement plan by maxing out the amount you can save? If not, what is it costing you?

_____

_____

_____

_____

_____

_____

7. Do you have enough money left over after paying bills and saving for the future that you can have some fun with your money and not feel guilty or stressed about it? How much "fun money" do you allow? Is it too much, not enough or just right for your budget?

_____

_____

_____

_____

_____

_____

EXERCISE 3: Answer these questions honestly.

1. If you need to make adjustments to balance your finances, what needs to stay and what can go? Begin with the necessities (your regular expenses such as utilities, rent/house payment, transportation, food, etc.). Then evaluate the "wants" such as

entertainment. (Do you really need 500 TV channels, season tickets to sporting events or concerts, the speedboat that you take out on the lake twice a year, the golf club membership that you never seem to have time to use, etc.? Do you need to buy expensive coffee every day or eat out multiple times each week?) This isn't fun, but is important in creating a balanced financial life!

NEEDS	WANTS

2. In which areas of your spending can you make improvements to find a balance that works for you? Maybe you don't need to totally eliminate an expense, but can find a way to modify it. (For example, maybe you could drive a more efficient vehicle, pay as you go at the golf course, buy tickets occasionally for sporting events or concerts instead of season tickets, sell the boat and rent one on occasion, reduce your cable TV package or your phone service. There is always a way to reduce without totally eliminating something you enjoy!)

_____

_____

_____

_____

_____

_____

_____

_____

3. Would you benefit from consulting a financial planner or financial coach to help you create the balance that works best for you? Or do

you know what you need to do, but haven't exercised the self-discipline to put it into action? Would support help you to follow through with your financial plan?

_____

_____

_____

_____

_____

4. Who can you call to get the information you need to create the financial balance that will give you peace of mind? What information would you need to create a balanced financial plan? How will you feel when you have created a financial plan that works with your values and goals? How soon are you willing to get what you need to make it happen?

_____

_____

_____

_____

_____

_____

_____

_____

_____

_____

_____

Taking control of your financial life through thoughtful evaluation and self-discipline will help you to see the abundance that surrounds you. We don't need lots of material things to achieve a balanced life. Often when we simplify, we find more balance. We live in a world of plenty.

"You must gain control over your money or the lack of it will forever control you."
—Dave Ramsey

Chapter 11: Discovering Spirituality

"Expect your every need to be met, expect the answer to every problem, expect abundance on every level, expect to grow spiritually."
— *Eileen Caddy*

"All you need to do to receive guidance is to ask for it and then listen."
—*Sanaya Roman*

Spirituality conjures up different feelings and images depending upon your background – your religious beliefs, cultural heritage, upbringing and perception. I was raised Catholic and there is an element of spirituality that is fundamental to Catholicism. There is also a line that seems to be drawn and, if you cross it, you could be in dangerous, possibly evil, territory.

I am grateful for my Catholic upbringing as it gave me a sense of connection to God and to the concept of the Holy Spirit. I have always been intrigued by the concepts of heaven, angels, spirit, miracles, wonders, and the afterlife. I have also been careful to keep some of my spiritual beliefs to myself so as not to cause controversy or disharmony. I feel strongly pulled toward the spiritual side of a religious practice, but have often questioned the manmade rules. As I have grown and evolved, I lean much less on the church for guidance and more on my inner wisdom, my spirit, God within.

I want to be clear that religion and spirituality are **not** the same. I had trouble understanding this concept as a child, but have come to understand it in a way that is useful to me. My family was involved in AA (Alcoholics Anonymous). There were people in the program who practiced various religious beliefs, but through AA, they shared a spiritual belief in a Higher Power which was supported through the 12 Steps. Those involved in the AA, Al-Anon, Ala-Teen and Adult Children of Alcoholics programs will be the first to tell you that these programs are spiritually based but are not religious.

You can experience spirituality through religion, but spirituality can be experienced without religion. In an article posted on **spiritualityhealth.com**, Rabbi Rami Shapiro wrote:

> *"Religion is often about who's in and who's out, creating a worldview steeped in 'us against them.' Spirituality rejects this dualism and speaks of us and them. Religion is often about loyalty to institutions, clergy, and rules. Spirituality is about loyalty to justice and compassion. Religion talks about God. Spirituality helps to make us godly. The two need not be at odds. Religion at its best is spirituality in community."*

In another article, the same author said:

> *"Religion is about belonging, community, shared values, shared rituals, and mutual support. Spirituality is about living life without a net, forever surrendered to reality and meeting each moment with curiosity, wonder, gratitude, justice, humility, and love. The two are not antithetical. Religion is often a container in which spiritual practices are preserved and passed on. Some people find the container as helpful as what it contains and choose to belong to a specific religion. Others simply take what they need from the containers and fashion their own way. I do a bit of both."*

The purpose of this chapter is not to have a religious debate, but to encourage you to think about how you experience and nurture your spirituality. You may incorporate religious practices into your life as a method of experiencing spirituality. My mother does this through saying the rosary daily. Some experience spirituality through nature and wonder. When I go walking outside or when we go on a vacation to a the mountains or the ocean, I always connect to my spirit and feel like I am part of something much larger and greater than I am. At the same time, I know that we are like parts of one body; we work together to keep the body running smoothly. No one part is more important than any other part. Just as in a human body, a brain cell and a fingernail cell are very different and are found in different organs and systems, but both are vital to the health and well-being of the whole. As a part of the system called the universe, we are all cells with different jobs that are vital to the health and well-being of the whole system. When we see ourselves as different yet vitally important, we understand how important it is that we don't judge one another as being of more or less importance. We are equally important, and we must work together to keep the system running smoothly. When we fight with one another, we are working against the very system upon which we all rely to sustain and nurture us. We destroy our universal body just as cancer cells fight healthy cells for dominance and destruction. Working together, we are strong. Fighting against one another, we destroy ourselves.

Spirituality through Prayer and Gratitude

"Your desire is our prayer. Picture the fulfillment of your desire now and feel its reality and you will experience the joy of the answered prayer."
—Dr. Joseph Murphy

Prayer is a common spiritual practice and can be experienced in a variety of settings. Churches, synagogues and temples are obvious locations for prayer, but I often find myself praying off and on all day long, regardless of my location. I may be at home, preparing dinner, doing dishes, or cleaning house when I find myself throwing up a prayer of gratitude for my family, my home, my health, my work, or just for being alive. When I am shopping, I am grateful for the wonderful healthy food choices we have in our country, in our state, in our city, and in our grocery stores. I am thankful for the hands that work to produce our food and get it to the stores so that I may buy

91

and prepare it for my family. When I am at work, I thank God for my clients and that they allow me into their lives to help them heal and create lives of meaning and purpose. I also thank God for my beautiful office that offers peace and tranquility to my clients and allows me to do my work in a calm, warm, and loving environment. When I am outside pulling weeds in the garden or walking around my neighborhood, I am grateful for nature, the miracles of life that occur daily with plants, animals, and even insects. (God bless them as they pollinate our gardens, flowers, and trees and also take care of other pests that may damage our plants.) When I drive, I find myself in prayer as I ask God to bless the walkers, bikers, other drivers, homeless people, children playing, police officers, and accident victims as I pass by. I pray at bedtime, thankful for another day and for all the people who touched my life that day. I ask for blessings on my family, friends, clients, the sick, the suffering, the dying, and, as I prayed with my son as he was growing up, "Bless all those who are less fortunate than we are." I do it so freely and naturally that I am not even aware of how frequently I pray. I know that it is a part of whom I am and I always feel connected to a power much greater than I, while knowing that greater power is a part of me.

Prayer can be formal, as in a church service or saying a memorized prayer such as The Lord's Prayer or The Serenity Prayer, but it is not limited to words that someone else has written. Prayer can be creative and spontaneous, free verse, if you are comparing to poetry. I was raised learning many formal prayers but find that I much prefer having a conversation with God throughout my day. I remember these words but can't tell you where I read them or heard them: "God is as near as a whispered prayer." I have spent much of my life with the idea that I can have a conversation with God anytime, anywhere. When I had a serious car accident on my way to church on Ash Wednesday in Apple Valley, California in 1987, my constant prayer from the moment I realized I was going to be hit was "Oh, God! Oh, God! Oh, God!" I was calling on a higher power to protect me and to be with me. I felt God's presence through the accident and through the earth angels who came to help me. From the teacher who got out of his car to make sure I was okay, to the ambulance crew who took me across the street to the hospital, to the X-ray technician who called a woman in to help me get undressed and to pray with me through the shock, to Martha, the teacher who took me back into her home because I couldn't navigate the stairs to my apartment while on crutches. As I write this, I still feel such gratitude that I find myself crying as if it just happened. My prayers were answered and moved me in such a way that I will always remember and be grateful. It strengthened my faith in the goodness of people and my belief that we are all connected in spirit.

EXERCISE 1: Have you experienced spirituality through prayer? Describe your experience.

_____

_____

_____

_____

_____

_____

The Serenity Prayer, authored by American theologian Reinhold Niebuhr is used in 12-Step Programs around the globe. It is short, succinct and extremely powerful. For those of you who are unfamiliar with it, here it is:

God, grant me the serenity to accept the things I cannot change,
Courage to change the things I can,
And wisdom to know the difference.

I offer this prayer to my clients, especially when they are frustrated with people, places, things or situations that are out of their control. It is a reminder to keep it all in perspective and to take control of what you can: yourself, your thoughts, your attitude, your feelings, and your actions. It is a reminder to let go of unreasonable expectations, as well as the hurt and anguish created as a result. This prayer works well in conjunction with another 12-Step Program saying, "Let Go and Let God." Step back and let God or a Higher Power step in.

EXERCISE 2: What prayers help you connect to your spiritual self? What type of prayers do you prefer, formal or informal? How, when and where do you pray?

_____

_____

_____

_____

_____

_____

EXERCISE 3: What role does gratitude play in your life? How do you practice or experience it?

_____

_____

_____

_____

_____

_____

Spirituality through Meditation

Meditation is similar to prayer, but doesn't require a lot of words. You may choose one or two words or syllables as a mantra that you repeat aloud or in your head. If you are doing a guided meditation, you may be given several words or a sentence to come back to when your mind wanders and starts running on the hamster wheel ("monkey mind" is another name for the mind running amok and out of control). You may choose to listen to meditative music or sounds that help you to relax. I enjoy nature sounds or soft meditative music with flutes, guitar, piano, and strings, or a combination of the nature sounds and gentle music. You may sit comfortably in a chair with your feet flat on the ground or cross-legged on the floor. In yoga, we sometimes get into "relaxation pose" lying on the floor with a light blanket on top to be comfortable while meditating and relaxing, but not to the point of falling asleep. If you are tired and think you may fall asleep, sit instead of lying down. I admit that sometimes when I am doing a guided meditation at bedtime, I fall asleep before it is over, so I try to be aware of my level of tiredness and do it earlier so I get the full benefit of the meditation I am listening to.

When I am in nature, I meditate on the wonders of all life and creation. I ponder. I experience a sense of awe and wonder. I observe the perfection that surrounds me. I am reminded of the Bible verse in Matthew 6:25-27 & 6:34: "Therefore I tell you, do not worry about your life, what you will eat or drink; or about your body, what you will wear. Is not life more important than food, and the body more important than clothes? Look at the birds of the air; they do not sow or reap or store away in barns, and yet your heavenly Father feeds them. Are you not much more valuable than they? Who of you by worrying can add a single hour to his life?" "So do not worry about tomorrow; for tomorrow will care for itself. Each day has enough trouble of its own."

EXERCISE 4: If you already know how to meditate, make it a regularly scheduled practice. If you have never tried it, give it a try. There are many resources available via the internet, cell phone apps, public libraries, book stores, health clubs, etc. Make it a point to gather some information or find a free resource to guide you through a meditation experience. I found a free cell phone app called "Pacifica" that offers meditations as well as guided breathing and guided relaxation. I also enjoy the Oprah & Deepak Chopra 21-Day Meditation Experiences. If you miss the free trials, you can order them through *chopracentermeditation.com*. Make a plan. When, where, and what meditation experience will you try?

_____
_____
_____
_____
_____
_____

I sometimes find myself in a meditative state when I am cleaning, doing something repetitive such as vacuuming, or washing dishes. I frequently find that I am meditating while I am doing something creative such as scrapbooking, making cards, or taking photos in nature. The same is true when I am cooking or baking which are also creative tasks. I lose track of time and become so involved with the act of creating that I feel at one with the universe and experience a state of peace, calm and joy.

Alone Time

"Women need real moments of solitude and self-reflection to balance out how much of ourselves we give away."
—*Barbara De Angelis*

Alone time can be a scary concept for some people. It is not to be confused with loneliness which means sadness because one has no friends or company. Alone time is time set aside to be <u>with yourself</u>. Consider it a date with a friend and that friend is you. Although we need time with others in order to feel connected, we also need time alone to get to know ourselves. This time can be spent meditating, reading, painting, drawing, journaling, or doing nothing. The last one is the one that I find most difficult as I am most comfortable doing something. I use my alone time in a variety of ways. I like to journal as it gives me a way to let go of and sort out all the thoughts dancing in my head. I usually gain insight into myself, my feelings and my desires, as I journal. I also love books, so setting aside time to read invigorates me. I enjoy doing anything creative, so I love taking time to work in my scrapbooking room. I especially enjoy it when nobody else is home to interrupt my alone time. For me, it is a form of meditation and I feel calm and peaceful as I create.

EXERCISE 5: Make a date with yourself for some alone time. Decide how you want to spend this time. Make a plan and enjoy this time with yourself! Remember that this is <u>not</u> the time to invite others to join you. Listen to your inner voice and hear what it tells you. How would your inner self like to spend this time? Just as you consider the needs of a friend, consider <u>your</u> needs as you choose how to spend this date with yourself.

_____

_____

_____

_____

_____

"Doing nothing" is not as easy as it sounds. When I was on bed rest during the last trimester of my pregnancy, I had to lie on my left side all day, except for bathroom breaks and 20 minutes for each meal. It was pure torture for a person who likes to accomplish things. I had to learn that taking time to do nothing was in fact, doing something. I was taking care of myself and my baby. Through this quiet time, I created a bond with my baby and with myself. I realized how important this time was and how much I had neglected taking good care of my basic needs before my pregnancy. I became very aware of my body, my baby, and my physical needs. I felt more in touch with my senses and became more observant. Now when I do nothing, it usually involves sitting outside on the swing in the little reading nook my husband made for me. I sit and listen to the birds, squirrels, and neighborhood dogs, and I pay attention to the temperature, the breeze, the sun and shade, and how it feels to sit and relax. I think or I completely clear my mind. I meditate. I pray. I breathe. I enjoy just being. I let go of schedules, lists and the need to do something. I close my eyes and feel my connection to the world and the universe.

EXERCISE 6: Carve out some time this week to do nothing. Put it in your schedule. Honor it and keep the date with yourself. Notice what you learn about yourself in this time. Notice how you feel. Journal about it.

_____

_____

_____

_____

_____

_____

_____

_____

_____

_____

_____

_____

Remember what my graduate school professor, Kent Estes, told me, "You are a human *being*, not a human *doing*." Take time to "be" in the moment.

Spirituality through Creativity

In addition to my own acts of creating, I enjoy art that others have created. Have you ever seen a work of art so beautiful that you got lost in it? I enjoy going to art museums when I can. I feel a sense of awe and wonder as I look at the pieces and allow myself the time to slow down and experience them, not only as an observer, but as the artists may have experienced the subjects. I love the colors, the textures, the brush strokes, the light and the shadows, the curves, the lines, patterns, and all of the details that I can take in. I am amazed that such beautiful pieces are created by human hands and believe that they are inspired by a spiritual connection that goes much deeper than good technique. I long to see the priceless masterpieces in Italy and Greece instead of seeing replicas.

Creativity takes many forms. Beautiful music can bring tears to my eyes. I have heard many young singers on TV or YouTube that sing like angels in children's bodies. My son is a talented musician who plays piano, violin, viola, percussion, and used to play saxophone. He has perfect pitch which is a rare gift and he understands music as a second language. There are times when I have heard him play with such emotion that tears come to my eyes, and I am amazed that such beautiful sounds can come from an instrument that his hands touch and manipulate. When I have these experiences, I feel connected to something deep within me and, at the same time, something that is far beyond me. I am reminded of a quotation by Pierre Teilhard de Chardin: "We are not humans having a spiritual experience but spiritual beings having a human experience."

EXERCISE 7: Consider the previous quote. What does it mean to you? How does creativity connect to spirituality in your life?

_____

_____

_____

_____

_____

_____

Back in our discussion on self-care, I mentioned a wonderful book by Julia Cameron. I highly recommend *The Artist's Way: A Spiritual Path to Higher Creativity*. It is written as a twelve-week course in "discovering and recovering your creative self." I mentioned the two basic tools Cameron says are non-negotiable: the morning pages and the artist's date. Let me explain them more thoroughly here.

The morning pages are three handwritten pages, strictly stream-of-consciousness whose main purpose is brain drain. Cameron says, "There is no wrong way to do morning pages." I tell my clients to keep a notebook near their bed and when they wake up in the morning, begin writing until they have filled three pages (front, back, front). Don't worry about spelling, punctuation, grammar, etc. Just write and give the critic in your head a voice (Julia calls the critic the "Censor," others call it "the Gremlin," "Monkey mind," etc.). When you acknowledge it and keep writing, you take away its power, freeing yourself to be more creative. Cameron says the reason for writing them is "to get to the other side... the other side of our fear, of our negativity, of our moods. Above all, they get us beyond our Censor. Beyond the reach of the Censor's babble we find our own quiet center, the place where we hear the still, small voice that is at once our creator's and our own." I love doing the morning pages! But I must admit that I didn't do them dutifully for years. I did them off and on and when I was doing them regularly, I thought I would keep doing them every day, forever. Then I allowed life in the form of family, work, exercise classes, other responsibilities, etc. to take the time that I would have spent writing. As I wrote this to share with you, I was drawn back to the morning pages and picked them back up because I have always found them a valuable practice.

The second tool Cameron says to commit to is the artist's date. This is a one to two-hour block of time that you set aside to do something creative, or to nurture your creativity. It is a play date that you preplan. This is time for you to get in touch with your creative side without others. Cameron says, "It doesn't have to cost anything but your time. You can do anything that is quality time." She gives examples of visiting a great junk store, a solo trip to the beach, watching an old movie, visiting an aquarium or art gallery, watching a sunrise or sunset, going to a different church to hear gospel music, visiting an ethnic neighborhood to taste foreign sights and sounds, bowling, a long country walk, etc. Look at it as a play date with your inner child/artist.

EXERCISE 8: I recommend buying *The Artist's Way* and following Julia Cameron's twelve-week course. If you don't want to do this, get a notebook and begin writing your morning pages. Notice the changes in how you feel and what you are able to accomplish.

EXERCISE 9: Commit to a two-hour block of time for your artist's date to play once a week for six weeks. Notice the difference in how you feel, how you are able to problem solve and your level of creativity. Pay attention to your spiritual connection and write about it.

_____

_____

_____

_____

_____

_____

_____

_____

_____

Spirituality through Knowledge and Inspiration

I love a good book! Regardless of whether hard bound, paperback, e-book or audio book, I love to learn and I love to read a variety of books. I find that reading good books inspires me to make a spiritual connection with myself, others, and the universe. When I find a good book, I pass the title along to clients, friends, family, and acquaintances I think may enjoy it. I sometimes leave a book in the waiting room of my office hoping that clients may pick it up and find something they can use in their lives. I give books away as gifts and keep a supply on hand for special occasions such as baby showers, birthdays or holidays. There is something uplifting about sharing these inspirational readings with others. I feel like it is my responsibility to help others, so I am often considering who else may benefit from something I am reading, and I share it with them. Whether they read it is up to them, but at least I feel like I have tried to make a positive impact in some small way. (You will find some of these titles in the Resource section at the end of this book.)

There are also spiritual videos, TV shows (such as Super Soul Sunday on Oprah's OWN network, Joel Osteen, etc.), movies, and podcasts (i.e. "Wayne Dyer on Hay House Radio" continues after his death). Tune in to some of these resources to give yourself a boost of inspiration. There are many uplifting programs available at no cost so check them out and get inspired!

EXERCISE 10: Find something interesting to learn about to connect to your spiritual side. Learn something new, through reading, watching or listening. Notice how you feel. Journal about it. See how it shows up in your life.

_____

_____

_____

_____

_____

_____

_____

_____

Intuition

"Every time you don't follow your inner guidance, you feel a loss of energy, loss of power, a sense of spiritual deadness."
—Shakti Gawain

"Never apologize for trusting your intuition. Your brain can play tricks, your heart can be blind, but your gut is always right."
—Rachel Wolchin

Have you ever had the experience of feeling like something wasn't right, but you tried to convince yourself that it was? Sometimes it is a long road between the heart and the brain and we try to think ourselves through a situation that we would be best to feel our way through. I think of intuition as "the voice of God within." It seems to me that we all have the innate ability to sense when we are in a dangerous situation. How many stories have you heard or experienced when somebody goes against their instincts and ends up in trouble? Scary movies often use this theme. I have had numerous clients who were in abusive relationships and regretted going against their instincts so that they ended up in situations they had difficulty getting out of. I encouraged them to pay attention to how they felt when they thought of walking into their home when the abuser was present and how they felt when that person wasn't there. If you feel sick to your stomach, nervous, scared, depressed, or your heart races, these are signs that you need to run. Just as our ancestors sensed the presence of a saber-toothed tiger and realized they needed to run or they would become dinner, we need to acknowledge that although another person may not be a saber toothed tiger, they can be just as dangerous and we need to muster up the courage and strength to run and hide for self-preservation.

Katelynn suspected her husband of cheating on her. He insisted that she was paranoid and was making something out of nothing. When she confronted him about the evidence she found in the bedroom, he made excuses claiming those things had been there for a long time and she just hadn't noticed them. She gave him specific examples of other things such as interactions on his Facebook account and text messages she saw on his phone. He twisted these things around to blame her for not trusting him. This caused her to question her sanity and her intuition, which was screaming at her to leave the situation. Katelynn went against her intuition one more time before finally listening to it and ending the relationship. She continued to question herself and her decision so we worked on helping her learn to pay attention to her physical body in different situations and with different people so she could get back in touch with her inner compass that would steer her in the right direction.

In my own life, I always find that when I am having trouble making a decision and I seek guidance from someone else, if they recommend something that goes against my instincts, I regret it if I take their recommendation. When we bought our commercial building and made plans for the décor, I found a carpet sample that had a bit of blue-grey thread in it. I thought I would use a slate blue for accent walls in the waiting room, the conference room, and my office. A friend told me that color would be too dark for the space, and I would be better to go with something lighter. I looked at other samples taking her idea into consideration and ended up choosing a lighter blue. I painted the first wall and didn't like it. I thought that it may look better if I let it dry so I painted the other two walls and still didn't like it. I ended up going back to the paint store and buying the blue I had originally selected, repainted all three walls, and was much happier. Nobody has told me it is too dark, but most importantly, I like it. It is a calm and soothing color which is exactly what I want in my waiting room, office, and conference room.

Another example occurred at an amusement park. We met another family at Worlds of Fun in Kansas City. I quit riding thrill rides years ago because as I got older, my stomach couldn't take it and I would get sick. Jane, the other mom, told me I should ride one of the big roller coasters with my son so he would have a memory of the two of us on a ride together. She continued to press me, so I went against my intuition and got on the giant roller coaster with my son to please her instead of listening to my inner wisdom and voice of experience. I'm sure you can tell how this ended up. I didn't throw up, but my son had to help me off the ride. I had trouble regaining my balance and I felt ill the rest of the day so I couldn't even enjoy the tame rides. What did I learn from this? I will never make a decision to please another person when I have to live with the negative consequences. It is okay to say "no" when somebody else makes a recommendation. Each of us must decide what is best for us and must listen to our own intuition.

I am going through the same decision-making process in choosing a title for this book. I had a title for it years ago, but the feedback I got on it was lukewarm so I began rethinking other possible titles. I came up with a list of 28 and have been getting feedback to narrow it down to four or five. I will get more feedback and will ultimately choose the title that I think best fits. I like getting other opinions, but we all need to recognize that we are responsible for the choices we make and nobody else has to live with them. It always comes back to making the best choice for you—not to please anybody else, but to please yourself!

Focus on your inner wisdom, the inner voice that tells you when something feels right or when it feels wrong. Notice how you feel in the pit of your stomach as well as any other physical signs. If you feel a smile and lightness, this is a sign that it may be right for you. If you feel sick to your stomach and dread the situation, this is a sign that you really <u>don't</u> want to do it—so listen and <u>don't</u> do it! Your intuition will never steer you wrong. It is your inner compass that always knows the right direction. If you go against it, you will get far off course, and it takes some time to get back on the path to your successful and balanced life.

My intuition helps me to navigate my life and it helps me to help my clients. I notice that when I get out of my head and go to my heart as I listen to my clients, I pick up on their feelings and can help them to tap into their intuition. I notice their body language, the slight hesitation in their voice, the change in their eye contact, the shift in the way they are sitting, the tension or relaxation in their body, and I make them aware of what I see and feel. Often, they are unaware of all the signals their body is giving them to say "Hey, listen to me, your intuition!" I bring them back to awareness and remind them that they have their own answers. They are found in their intuition, if they just quiet themselves and listen.

EXERCISE 11: What do you think of when you hear the word "intuition"? How do you feel about it? With what do you associate "intuition"? Do you believe that we all have it and can use it? Have you experienced a time when you went against your intuition? How about a time when you heeded that inner voice? How did you feel in each situation?

_____

_____

_____

_____

_____

_____

_____

_____

Notice when you are aware of knowing something you didn't know that you knew. (How's that for a confusing request?) What I mean is to pay attention to your inner voice and notice how often it shows up. Notice how you feel when you pay attention and are aware of it. Do you listen to it? Or do you ignore it? Be still and listen to your inner wisdom.

"What I am actually saying is that we need to be willing to let our intuition guide us, and then be willing to follow that guidance directly and fearlessly."
—_Shakti Gawain_

Chapter 12: Reclaiming Fun

"Dance as though no one is watching you; love as though you have never been hurt before, sing as though no one can hear you, live as though heaven is on earth."
—Alfred Souza

Have you ever watched small children at play? They become engrossed in their imaginations and creativity, and they instinctively know how to have fun! Think about it; do you have to teach children how to play or do they teach you? If you are a willing participant, children will dress you up, tell you what role to play, what words to say, and how to act the part they want you to play. They have a clear picture of what is supposed to happen and if you try to deviate from their script, they will tell you. My friend and former professor, Paul Welter, Ed.D., wrote a book, taught a class, and had a radio show entitled "Learning from Children" whereby he encouraged adults to play like children and to learn how to have fun with children as our teachers. Think of a time when you were playing with a child and you were not fully engaged. Maybe you were distracted by your phone, the TV, your own thoughts, etc. What happened? Did the child tell you to pay attention to them and the game at hand?

Once when my son was three years old and wanted to play with me, I had the TV on and was watching the news. He was handing me toys and trying to get me to engage in his play, but I was only half-heartedly participating. He took my face in his tiny hands, looked me directly in the eyes and said, "Mommy, TV off!" That was a wake-up call to me to focus on what was really important, and it was not the news. I was missing out on precious time with my son because I was keeping an eye on the TV instead of turning it off and giving him my full attention. TV time may be enjoyable, but it is <u>not</u> precious! Time with a three year old, on the other hand <u>is</u> precious and ends much too soon.

As a child, I knew how to have fun and entertain myself. I played outside with my siblings, uncle and friends. We played touch football, tetherball, badminton, tag, and hide and seek. We rode our bicycles around town and swam at the swimming pool every day when it was open. We ran through sprinklers, played with our kittens and puppies, climbed trees, jumped in the fall leaves, made snowmen, snow angels and snow forts. We raided Gram's garden for strawberries and her orchard for raspberries after swimming. We played board games like Monopoly, Aggravation, Chinese Checkers, Dominoes, Chess, Clue, Tiddlywinks, and Checkers. We played card games such as 10-Point Pitch, Uno, Peanuts, and Solitaire. I read a lot of books and especially enjoyed the mystery series of Nancy Drew books, The Encyclopedia Brown books, *The Phantom Tollbooth,* and anything at all about magic. I liked to draw and color and taught myself how to play the Magnus Chord Organ which used a number system instead of the letter system for notes. As a teenager, I enjoyed school activities such as music and theatre and looked for any excuse to wear a costume. I was often referred to as "bubbly," which really meant that I enjoyed what I was doing and was present in the moment. I'm sure the positive experiences I had as a babysitter and as a student influenced my decision to become a teacher. I was playful and saw teaching as a way to continue to have fun while I was working.

When I became a school counselor, I noticed a shift in my demeanor and in how I approached work and life. My job was focused on problems and I became more serious. It became more difficult for me to have fun. My son was a great teacher and reminded me often that I needed to take time for fun. As adults, we easily forget how important it is to make fun a priority in our lives. This is where we can take a lesson from children. We need to forget our grown-up problems for a little while and laugh and have fun, like we did when we were children!

> *"If it's not fun, you're not doing it right."*
> *—Bob Basso*

EXERCISE 1: Think back to your childhood. What did you do that was fun?

_____

_____

_____

_____

_____

_____

With whom did you have fun? Siblings? Friends? Parents? Grandparents? Contact at least one of these people and invite them to get together to do an activity you used to have fun doing together.

_____

_____

_____

What made these activities fun for you?

_____

_____

_____

_____

_____

When was the last time you engaged in one of these activities you loved as a child or teen? Describe it.

_____

_____

_____

_____

_____

What has prevented you from doing these fun activities in the past? Explain.

_____

_____

_____
_____
_____
_____

Do you miss these fun activities?
_____

What prevents you from doing them now?
_____
_____
_____
_____
_____
_____

How would you feel if you removed the obstacles that kept you from engaging in these fun activities?
_____
_____
_____

What would it take to remove one or more of the obstacles so you could enjoy a childhood activity?
_____
_____
_____
_____
_____
_____

If you get stuck as you try to think of fun activities, it helps to not only look at childhood activities but also to consider activities you participated in as a young adult. (Let me be clear. I am not advocating breaking laws, endangering yourself or others or doing anything that would in any way harm yourself or anybody else. I am not encouraging inappropriate behavior of any kind. So if you were the type of kid who drank alcohol or used drugs as a teen, these are not the activities I am referring to. I am also not encouraging reckless driving, theft, etc. These behaviors cause harm to self and others so don't even entertain these ideas. Keep it clean and positive!) The activities I want you to consider may be sports you participated in (golf, running, basketball, baseball, volleyball, swimming, etc. – something you could still do today, maybe modified), or playing a musical instrument, or giving speeches, performing in plays, sewing, gardening, cooking, writing poetry or short stories, reading, building with Legos, putting model cars together, woodworking, jigsaw puzzles, playing chess or other board games, doing card tricks, singing, dancing, watching movies, riding bikes, fishing, hunting, playing pool, pinball, watching sporting events live, talking with friends, drawing, painting, sculpting, crocheting, knitting, cross stitching, crafts, photography, playing with pets, cards, badminton, canoeing, camping, cooking out at a park, watching wildlife, swimming in the river or lake, or going for a long drive just to enjoy the scenery, etc. The list goes on and on.

EXERCISE 2: Think back to hobbies you have had, either indoors or outdoors, as a child, teen or adult. What is one hobby that you miss and would enjoy doing again?

_____

_____

_____

What equipment would you need? Do you already have it? Maybe it is stored in a box or tub that you could easily access. Is it an investment of time or money? How can you find the resources you need?

_____

_____

_____

_____

_____

_____

Consider activities you have fun doing alone, as well as those you enjoy doing with others. Some activities such as board games are much more fun with others. Artistic hobbies are sometimes more fun to do alone. I enjoy writing by myself as it requires thought and I don't want to be interrupted. I can enjoy photography with others, such as my family when we are on vacation, but I can take my time and set up photos more creatively when I am alone. Fun can be had alone or with others so having a variety on your "Menu of Fun Activities" will broaden your options and will help you to match the activity according to the time available, others that are available or not, and your mood – what you feel like doing.

EXERCISE 3: Create your **Menu of Fun Activities**. Just as a restaurant menu has different categories, you may create categories for your activities (i.e. Go It Alone, 1-2 Buddies, Small Group, Large Group, Indoor, Outdoor, Athletic, Creative, etc.). Make your list of Categories. You may set up a spreadsheet or use a piece of paper. You can type it up like a restaurant menu to make it more fun. You can be as artistic as you want. Remember that it should be fun!!

Once you have created your Menu, choose at least one item from the Menu to try this week. Consider the time involved, who you will invite (if it is an activity for more than one person), what, if any, supplies are needed and the cost. Get everything in place, put it in your schedule and keep it sacred! Don't let anything get in the way of your fun time this week! Enjoy!

Creative Fun

"You can't use up creativity. The more you use, the more you have."
—*Maya Angelou*

We talked about creativity as part of spirituality, but I want to revisit it here. We are designed to be creative, and creativity should be joyful and fun! Look at small children and notice how they love to create! They don't care about the final product but enjoy the process of making something—anything!

Creativity requires us to engage our imagination. Again, we'll look to children for inspiration. Give a child a stick and they will find a creative use for it. They may wave it around like a magic wand or swing it like a bat or use it to dig a hole in the sand. Give them a hose and some dirt and see what they do with it. The possibilities are endless! Mud pies, castles, roads, caves, tunnels, landscapes, new worlds of possibilities are available when they use their creativity and imagination. Kids will make up songs, dances, plays and stories. They will create their own costumes out of simple things they find, such as blankets, towels, plastic containers, pots and pans, boxes, paper and old shoes or boots. Notice the delight on their faces as they engage in creative play! They are involved in pure joy and fun! They want the grumpy grown-ups to join in so they can share the joy that they experience. This can be a challenge for many adults who are much more comfortable in observation than in participation.

EXERCISE 4: As an adult, are you a participant or an observer? Consider this question as it relates to your own creative desires as well as playing with children.

_____

_____

_____

_____

_____

_____

Do you play creatively? Do you invite others to play with you? Do you become fully engaged in your creativity? Or do you watch others play for fear of judgment? How can you get off the sidelines and become more fully engaged with your own creativity?

_____

_____

_____

_____

_____

_____

Interests

"In between goals is a thing called life that has to be lived and enjoyed."
—Sid Caesar

Some people may have difficulty thinking of activities as "fun" so let's consider the concept of "interests" as a different way to look at it. Think about the topics that interest you; the books, TV shows or movies that capture your attention. When you go on vacation, where are the places you put on the list as "must see"? What would you like to learn more about when you have time?

I am interested in genealogy, family history, and stories about my ancestors. I would like to spend more time researching my family, so when we get together, I find myself interviewing my aunts and uncles, my mother, and any other relatives interested in sharing information about our family. I have my grandmother's scrapbooks, photo albums, slides, family Bibles, and newspaper clippings. I have found letters that were preserved in the envelopes and stored inside the pages of a Bible. I have found report cards of my father, uncles, and grandmother, as well as baby books and shot records. There are ribbons won at county fairs for vegetables, canned goods, and showing sheep. I found my grandmother's nursing degree and official photo with her nursing cap. I look at these things and seek the stories behind them. Gram kept travel journals, which told of the daily activities as she traveled to places such as Niagara Falls, Yosemite National Park, Germany, Australia, and New Zealand. I am grateful that I have some of her stories in her handwriting as it gives me some insight into her interests and experiences. I can easily lose track of time when I start going through these things and doing my research. This is fun for me.

My husband also enjoys family history and is fortunate enough to have relatives who put together books from all four branches of his family (his grandparents on both sides). These books show photos, tell stories, show family trees, have marriage and death records, maps, and land ownership information. He has recently been contacted by a relative who is researching her family and found that he is a DNA match. He is also very interested in history, especially war history. When we travel, he likes to stop and read historical markers and visit old battlegrounds. He says he wants to spend more time reading about history when he retires.

We have some relatives who are interested in quilting and the stories behind the quilts. Some quilts have been passed on for generations and may be a bit worn out, but they have history and meaning to the family. We happen to have a Quilt Museum in Lincoln that is a part of the University and is a treasure to those interested in quilting.

Recipes are another area of interest for many people. When my grandmother died, my aunts wanted desperately to find certain recipes, such as the one for Northland Cookies. I met a young woman at a writing workshop who is tracing the journey of the family recipes she inherited. She would like to know the stories behind the recipes. Do recipes hold any interest for you?

My father-in-law had lots of interests and spent much time collecting things related to those interests. As a geologist, he attended rock and mineral shows and collected rocks and gems, especially agates and amethysts. He enjoyed antique cars so he had a Model A Victoria restored. He also had his father's Thunderbird, a small convertible, a postal wagon and a steam engine. He enjoyed traveling to steam engine and tractor shows and had a number of friends with similar interests. They enjoyed getting together to talk about trains and cars or to steam up an old engine.

I recently joined the Nebraska Writers' Guild and am excited about upcoming activities related to writing, as well as meeting like-minded people. I attended a Writers' Workshop recently and plan to attend a conference. One of my degrees is in English, so I am renewing my interest in writing by finding people with similar interests.

EXERCISE 5: What is fun for you in the area of interests or research?

_____
_____
_____
_____
_____

What do you have an interest in but haven't made the time to research or explore? What is one small step you could take in the next week to explore this interest? (It may be looking up information on the internet or at a library, contacting someone who knows about it, finding a museum that is related to your interest, reading a book or watching a TV show about it.)

_____

_____

_____

_____

_____

Try out different interests. Explore until you find one (or two, or three) that you enjoy thinking about and researching. Remember this in not a school assignment, this is for fun!

Chapter 13: Getting Away

"I think recharging is important, absolutely. Every now and then, you need maybe a couple of weeks to just chill out and let your emotions balance themselves out a little bit."
—Malin Akerman

"I think taking vacations and turning off the phone and only doing emails or social (media) for a specific short amount of time helps with work/life balance. If I'm checking it all day I start to feel cuckoo-bird. So I just do it once or twice a day instead of a thousand. And then remembering that it doesn't matter. It just doesn't matter."
—Maria Bamford

When was the last time you had a vacation? I'm not talking about a weekend away, but a real vacation—one that required actual time off from work. Are you aware of the number of Americans who don't use their paid vacation days? I was reading an article from *forbes.com* entitled "Why America's Overstressed Workers Won't Take a Break" that mentioned the fact that in 2016, Americans left a record 662 million vacation days unused. One third of all unused vacation days are forfeited. A similar article cited a study from *Hotwire* that reported "87% of Americans would take more vacation trips if they felt they had the time and the money to do so." Many people are afraid to take time off because they fear losing their jobs, but what is the cost of not taking vacation time? Employers end up with unhappy, stressed out, and unhealthy employees. People who don't take vacation end up having more health issues, including an increased chance of heart disease.

The cost of not taking vacation is high for both employers and employees. Productivity increases when employees have had time off. There is lower turnover when employees are less stressed. Health care costs and time off for illnesses are lower when people take vacations. Our immune system is boosted when we have time to unwind and not work. I always feel more relaxed, less stressed, more refreshed, and ready to get back into my work when I return from a vacation. This is reflected in some writing I did while we were on a short ski vacation in Wyoming.

Relaxation. Ahhh... Don't you just love the sound of it? It causes me to want to take a deep breath, let it all out, and actually relax. I am sitting in a ski lodge in Wyoming watching my family ski and watching my son's friend take ski lessons. I have taken pictures and videos of them so they can enjoy them later. The sun is bright and reflects off the fresh snow, blinding me when my sunglasses are off. The evergreen trees have small tufts of snow on their branches and look lovely. It is the first day of spring and we know this may be our last chance to enjoy the beauty of a white wonderland until later this year when fall and winter come back to Nebraska. We have a cooler filled with snacks and drinks to enjoy when the skiers take breaks.

We are staying in a nice hotel with lots of amenities. It is very comfortable and allows me a break so I don't have to worry about all the household chores. I was able to go to bed early last night and sleep in this morning. Breakfast was provided at the hotel so I didn't have to prepare anything or do the dishes.

I love coming out here, even though I don't ski. I love the beautiful mountain scenery and the time to write and read without a lot of interruptions. Internet and cell phones don't work out here, so I truly get a break from being connected to the rest of the world. It is a brief time to unplug and to replenish myself.

I find myself wondering why I don't schedule more opportunities like this to relax. I am a busy person by design. It's is in my make-up and I am not always very good at turning it off. But when I do, I love it! I have learned that I need to regularly schedule relaxation time or I will become exhausted and will burn out. As much as I love my life and accomplishing things, I need time to unwind, unplug and not think about work, chores, or other responsibilities. When I take time out, I go back to my life with a fresh outlook, renewed energy and creativity. I accomplish much more after a break than I do when I pound out work, day after day, week after week, month after month.

There are times when I take a "staycation." I stay at home while my family does an activity that I am not interested in doing. I love these breaks, too, because I don't have to cook, clean, do laundry or dishes and nobody else needs my help or attention. But it is different than getting away. When I stay at home, I don't fully relax because I have constant reminders of things that need to be done. I am still "on call" and sometimes I get sidetracked from relaxation. When I am traveling, nobody expects me to be available. We aren't creating dirty dishes and I don't have to go shopping for groceries. I am free to focus on the scenery, having fun with my family, reading books, and yes, even unread magazines that have accumulated on my coffee table! When I choose to work, it is writing, which is also fun and relaxing for me so doesn't feel like work. When I get a taste of relaxation, I want more! We only have a few days, then it is time to head back to the real world. We will listen to a Harry Potter book as we drive, one last chance to escape into a world that doesn't have chores and work waiting. I am grateful to have one more shot at blissful relaxation before arriving at home.

EXERCISE 1: Contemplate and write about the following questions: What do you do to relax? When was the last time you truly got away and relaxed? How did you feel before, during and after? What are the benefits to taking time off and vacationing?

_____
_____
_____
_____
_____
_____
_____
_____
_____
_____
_____
_____
_____
_____
_____
_____

EXERCISE 2: Consider where you would like to go for a vacation or a weekend getaway. What would you need to do to plan this vacation? Consider the details. When, where, what, with whom, how long? How much will it cost? Do you need to save money for it? Do you need to find somebody to fill in for you at work or give your boss notice of the dates you will be gone?

_____
_____
_____
_____
_____
_____
_____
_____

I hope you take some time to schedule your next relaxation getaway, even if it is in your own backyard!

"Life is all about balance. You don't always need to be getting stuff done. Sometimes it's perfectly okay, and absolutely necessary, to shut down, kick back, and do nothing."
—Lori Deschene

Chapter 14: Continuing to Learn

"Education is the most powerful weapon which you can use to change the world."
—Nelson Mandela

Education is a broad topic that covers formal education and life experience. People often throw around phrases such as life lessons, school of life, and he's about to get educated in reference to an event that may have an impact on how one sees their life. This doesn't have anything to do with college classes or degrees earned, but it is still education. One of the best things you can do to expand your brain and to keep yourself actively engaged is to learn new things. Take a foreign language class, learn how to play chess, take golf lessons, learn how to swim or scuba dive. Studies have shown a connection between learning new things and a reduction in depression. Learning is a way to keep the brain sharp so it doesn't atrophy. An article in The *New Yorker* listed many unexpected benefits to learning a new skill, including improving working memory, better verbal intelligence, and increased language skills. The more you practice the new skill, the easier it becomes. By learning new things, you strengthen the brain which can help to ward off dementia. Learning helps you keep life in balance.

I am a self-proclaimed "learn-a-holic." I became a teacher, in large part, due to my love for learning. As a teacher, I knew that I would forever be learning new things to teach my students and to grow as a professional educator. As a professional counselor, I am required to earn 32 CEU's (continuing education units) every two years to keep my license current. I can earn these credits by taking college credit classes, through workshops, professional reading and tests, webinars or videos, or through teaching workshops or classes. Although I would most likely take classes, read and attend workshops on my own, I appreciate that they are required as a standard in my professional life. It keeps me on my toes and requires that I continually strive for improvement as a counselor and life coach.

Personal growth is huge for me! I love to learn and grow. The more I learn, the more I want to learn. I am insatiable! I have a huge library of personal and professional books. You will find books in every room in my house as well as in my professional office. I listen to audio books while I drive, I own a Nook and I have Kindle books on my phone and computer. Wherever I go, I have access to reading material that challenges me to think and to grow. Much of my reading serves dual purpose, as I use it personally and professionally. I recommend books to clients, family, and friends frequently. I just can't get enough!

The old saying about "sharpening the saw" is a reminder to schedule time for yourself so you can be energized and are prepared to give 100 percent to the various aspects of your life. Education is the key to "sharpening your saw." The fact that you are reading this book shows that you are ready to learn something new and that you want to find ways to improve your life by finding balance in all areas.

Formal Education

Our son is in his third year of college. He went through three majors in three semesters and feels like he has found a major that matches his personality and preferences. It isn't easy to decide what you want to be when you grow up (I'm still working on it), and there is a lot of pressure for 17- and 18-year-olds to figure it out before they go to college or have enough life experience to make such a big decision. So why bother with education?

Formal education gives us tools to earn a living as well as to navigate the adult world. In addition to training you for a career, you meet people and have experiences that educate you in other ways. When you have roommates, you learn about different lifestyles and habits. You discover that not all people are the same as you. You learn how to negotiate who gets to choose the TV shows on the one TV that everybody uses, or what the others do when one roommate wants to have people over for dinner. Cleaning chores have to be divided up fairly. Laundry facilities must be shared, so you must determine who buys the detergent and other supplies. How are meals handled? Does each person do their own thing or do you shop and cook together? How do you divide the refrigerator and freezer space? What about dishes, and pots, and pans? Do you share or does each person use their own? Living in a dorm gives you similar experiences, but with a little more support. In either case, college is an opportunity to learn about adult responsibilities in a different environment than the growing-up home and family you are used to. It gives you a chance to try some things out before being totally on your own.

What about the expense? Is the cost of education worth the benefit? People want to believe that a formal education equates to more income throughout life. That doesn't mean that everybody requires a Bachelor's Degree or Master's Degree to be successful and to make a decent living. Many high-paying careers require trade school to learn a craft or skill. Even if people already have a skill they have learned from somebody else or have taught themselves, an associate's degree or certification can provide credentials and open doors. I dated a mechanic who went to a community college to get a certificate that said he was a mechanic even though he already had the skill and was doing the work. He wasn't thrilled that he had to take basic studies such as English because it wasn't relevant to fixing engines. But in taking classes not directly related to his work, he was exposed to some experiences that may have helped in his career in ways that he didn't see at the time. He needed the certificate to show he had the credentials to be employed by an auto repair shop. Was it worth the cost? I believe he would say it was. He later opened his own shop and had a great reputation for being one of the best mechanics in his town.

So how does formal education relate to balance? When you are training for a career that you are excited about, you are looking at a very important part of a balanced life. People who enjoy their work carry that happiness over into other areas of their lives. They experience less stress overall because they enjoy their work.

Choosing a career that matches with who you are is one of the critical choices you make in creating a balanced life. Is it any wonder that 17- and 18-year-olds feel so much stress about this decision? Many of them have observed adults who are dissatisfied with their work and they know they don't want to feel that way. If they have been around adults who love their work, they can see how it creates balance and happiness. If you have been trained for a career that you don't love, consider how much more centered and content you would be if you were able to use your knowledge and skills in an area that matches your values. It's never too late to find a career that helps you to create balance in your life.

Lifelong Learning

Some people say, "I am too old to learn" or "school was never my thing." I challenge you to reconsider these negative messages. Recently I heard about a woman in her mid-80s who had just earned her Bachelor's Degree. If she isn't too old to learn, neither are you. I have a friend who is retired and began taking writing classes for fun. He is now working toward a Master's Degree! You learn new things every day of your life, whether you want to or not. Maybe you learn something about a friend that you didn't know before, or maybe you learn a new recipe, or a new way to do something that is more efficient than the way you have always done it. People are constantly learning how to use a new phone app or how to do something new on their computer. Think about it; what is something you know today that you didn't know last week or last month? As long as we are living, we are learning! It doesn't have to be drudgery, but can be fun!

Many children and adults make huge sacrifices for the opportunity to learn and to attend school. Some will walk miles to get to the only school that they could possibly attend. The school may only be a small area with no desks, chairs, books or chalkboards, but they show up, eager and ready to learn! How can you find the same sense of excitement and enthusiasm about learning?

In this age of technology, it is easy to take free online classes, webinars and workshops, and watch videos that teach us a skill. You don't have to earn a degree to take classes. You can learn any practical, useful, or fun skill somewhere, if you just do some research. Community colleges and craft stores offer classes for fun like art or painting. When my son was young, we took a couple of pottery classes at a shop and made a mug for Dad, decorative fish, and a platter. You can take a class related to a hobby such as gardening or photography. You can take something for personal growth like a class on meditation or spirituality. What about learning to play an instrument like the guitar or piano? You may learn some of the basics from an online video and can graduate to taking lessons from a teacher. If you are interested in health and wellness, you can take a nutrition or cooking class, or try a yoga or exercise class. When my husband and I bought a commercial building and were doing some of the renovations ourselves, I watched a YouTube video to get some tips on how to lay tile. There are numerous classes on computer programs such as how to create a spreadsheet or a data base to print address labels. My point is that there is no reason or excuse to keep you from learning something you want to learn!

I like to learn about spiritual connections and appreciate tools that help get a deeper understanding of who I am and how I am connected to the universe. Learning is fun for me and always has been. Yes, I am the nerd who liked homework assignments. It gave me a chance to ponder the lesson and to gain a deeper understanding of what was taught. By offering exercises at the end of each chapter, I am giving you the same opportunity to integrate the reading with your personal experience to help you to gain a deeper understanding of yourself and to help you to contemplate how you can use the information to create more balance and meaning in your own life.

EXERCISE 1: How can education enhance your life?

_____
_____
_____
_____
_____
_____

What is something that you have wanted to learn but haven't taken the time to do it? What is the first step you would need to take to move toward learning this?

_____
_____
_____
_____
_____

How will you feel when you take the first step toward this learning goal?

_____
_____
_____
_____

How will you feel when you have completed this class, learned the skill, reached this learning goal, etc.?

_____
_____
_____
_____

How will this help you to create more balance in your life?

_____
_____
_____
_____
_____
_____

Chapter 15: Creating Your Environment for Success

"I'd like to propose a new definition of organization: 'Organizing is the process by which we create environments that enable us to live, work, and relax exactly as we want to. When we are organized, our homes, offices, and schedules reflect and encourage who we are, what we want, and where we are going.'"
—*Julie Morgenstern in her book,* <u>Organizing from the Inside Out</u>

Have you ever walked into a space that caused you to feel relaxed, or energized, or depressed? Too many of us discount our surroundings as a factor in achieving personal or professional goals. I want you to consider the possibility that our surroundings can set us up for success or failure.

What comes to mind when you think of the word "environment?" Most of us think of the outdoors, pollution, laws and regulations. It is true that these are all included in our environment, but what about our immediate surroundings? Have you ever considered that we are not only stewards of the outdoor environment, but also of our indoor environment? Most of us don't have homes that need to be condemned based on laws and regulations, but what about cleaning up our indoor environment to improve health and mood, and to increase production?

Hoarding has received a lot of publicity in recent years, so much so that there are TV shows that highlight the lives of hoarders and their efforts to clean up their environment for health and safety reasons. Our homes may not reflect such extremes, but I believe most of us would feel less stress and more balanced if we cleaned and organized our home and work environments. It may be as small as a kitchen drawer that needs to be tidied up, or it may be as large as a steel storage building which requires a lot of downsizing and cleaning out.

I had a client who had accumulated so much stuff in her home that tiny paths were the only way to navigate from one room to another. Her family tried to help her by moving as much of the clutter as possible to one room, packed from floor to ceiling, but it didn't eliminate the problem. We needed to explore what was happening within her that caused her to fill her life with stuff instead of what she really wanted and needed in order to feel full. Buying stuff that you don't need and can't afford will never fill you up. Holding onto possessions from loved ones who have passed on will not bring them back. Keeping something just in case you might need it someday is not a good reason to hang onto it and all of the stress that goes along with storing it.

EXERCISE 1: Look within and ask yourself, "What do I really want in my life that I am not getting? How can I get what I really want? What do I need to do to create the space for what I really want? What can I eliminate that is holding me back from the life I really want?"

_____
_____
_____
_____
_____
_____
_____
_____
_____
_____

After you answer these questions, take a look at your surroundings and do the following exercise:

EXERCISE 2: Take a few minutes to consider one area in your living environment that causes you stress. Is there a drawer, a closet, a room that you are ashamed of others seeing so you keep the door closed, or a desk that is so cluttered you can't see the desktop? Choose one small thing that you can do to clean up this part of your environment. Then do it immediately. Notice how you feel and journal about it. (You will probably need more space than is given here.)

_____

_____

_____

_____

_____

_____

_____

"Rome wasn't built in a day" and neither did your environment become messy and cluttered overnight. Be kind and patient with yourself as you tackle one small thing at a time. Give yourself credit for every small action you take to clean up your environment and celebrate each victory so you keep the momentum going. The cumulative effect of these small actions will eventually lead to feeling lighter, less stressed, happier and more content.

EXERCISE 3: You will create the environment you envision. Take the time to envision the environment you want and maybe even draw a picture of it. When you plan it out and can see it in your mind, you can bring it into reality. Notice how you feel when you close your eyes and imagine the environment that allows you to feel stress-free, productive, and creative. That is the feeling that you are going for. That is the payoff! Once you create this space, you will experience that feeling every time you are in that environment, creating energy and productivity! Journal about your vision for your new and improved environment.

_____

_____

_____

_____

_____

_____

_____

_____

_____

EXERCISE 4: As you start cleaning up your environment, take the time to assess everything in that space. Ask yourself, "Why is this here? Do I use it? Is this the right place for it? Do I love it?" If it isn't useful or something that enhances your enjoyment of the space, get rid of it.

If somebody else can use it or enjoy it, give it away or donate it. If it is broken or obsolete, throw it out. I am environmentally conscious, so I always consider donating items first. It is more difficult for me to throw something out if I think there is a possibility that somebody could use it. If I am having difficulty deciding what to do with an item, I consult with someone who can help me to realistically assess whether or not anybody else could or would use it. If I decide to throw it out, I decide if all or part of it can be recycled first. Then I throw out the remainder. Try it out. You will feel better no matter what you decide to do with the items. If you decide to keep something because you use it or love it, you may enjoy it more as a result of assessing its value to you. If you donate it, you will enjoy the feelings you get from helping others. If you recycle it, you can enjoy the feelings that come from being a good steward of our natural and physical environment. If you throw it out, you can enjoy the feelings that come from letting go of things that are no longer useful or meaningful, and the space that you have created in your life.

The great thing about tackling one thing at a time is that is isn't so daunting that you feel disabled or disheartened. When we walk, we must take one step at a time. At the beginning of a journey we may not be able to see the destination. We can't skip all the steps and magically arrive there. But if we take one step at a time, we will see our destination coming closer and clearer. We may pick up the pace, but we still must put one foot in front of the other to get there. So take it one step at a time. Choose a drawer, a shelf, a closet, a desktop and eventually you will have a room completed. Take time to celebrate this accomplishment, then move on to another room and take it one step at a time. Every step you take is one step closer to your destination. Keep your vision in mind and know that you will arrive!

Clutter

My Dad had a sign in his office that said, "A clean desk is a sign of a sick mind." He thought it was funny and used it as rationale for his messy office and desk. He had stacks of paperwork at least two-feet deep covering his entire desk! There was no work space available for him to sit at his desk and actually work on a project. He cleaned his desk once and it made the local newspaper, complete with photographs! It didn't last long. The piles soon returned and we didn't see the desktop again during his lifetime.

Although we can see the humor in this story, I hope we can also agree that it is rather sad. I wonder how much more productive Dad could have been if he had set up systems for filing and clearing his desk regularly. He didn't have a computer and did things the old fashioned way, with paper and pencil. There is nothing wrong with using paper and pencil, but you need to have a system for organizing and keeping track of the paperwork. When you create a system, it is easier to stay on top of things and to quickly and easily find the items you need when you need them. Clutter creates chaos and brings on feelings of stress and anxiety. Do you have a space in your life that you avoid because it is cluttered and it brings you down when you enter it? Some have the legendary junk drawer full of odds and ends of receipts, coupons, screws, nails, paperclips, tape, tools, pencils that need to be sharpened, pens that don't work, keys that nobody knows where they came from or what they belong to, puzzle pieces and broken pieces of various objects. Does this sound familiar?

Some people not only have a junk drawer but they may have a junk closet. Think of the TV shows that show somebody opening the dreaded messy closet. What happens? Everything falls out of the closet engulfing the person who opened it. It's a great sight gag and makes for a good laugh, as long as it is somebody else. It's not so funny when it is in your home and you are the one who gets lost in the pile of closet rubble.

Maybe a drawer or closet isn't enough space for your clutter. Maybe you have a room that has become the catch all. You avoid it and keep the door closed so you don't have to see it, or worse yet, so company won't see it. The thought of others seeing your clutter can cause stress and anxiety, and changes your behavior. For example, maybe you like to entertain or have guests over for dinner occasionally, but you realize that it has been weeks, months, or even years since you have invited anybody over because of the dreaded messy room. How sad to let clutter cheat you out of a part of life that you enjoy.

I've had numerous clients who were referred to me due to their cluttered environment and the stress it was causing in their lives and in the lives of those who cared about them. Clutter was creating health issues for some so action needed to be taken. One client, a woman in her early 60s that I will call Irene, lived alone in a house with four cats. She was referred by a social worker who had been trying to motivate her to clean up the space and was concerned about depression and health issues. I made a home visit with the social worker and wasn't quite prepared for what I saw. Cats had free reign and were on top of cupboards, counters and the kitchen table, wherever they could find a spot that wasn't filled with dirty dishes, rotten food, paper, boxes, or other clutter. The house smelled of cat urine so it was obvious that litter boxes hadn't been cleaned and they were using the carpet and other places instead. Fur was everywhere and there was no place to sit on any furniture because it was covered with clutter. Irene had gotten a new recliner and sat in it all the time. Her bedroom was such a mess that she couldn't get to the bed to clean it off and sleep in it, so she slept in the recliner, which was causing health issues. There was clothing piled everywhere. The social worker's ankles had been bitten by bugs while in this house. Irene was so depressed that she was paralyzed into non-action. She was so overwhelmed with clutter that she couldn't even begin to clean it up! So she sat in her recliner, drank pop, ate junk food and escaped into the imaginary world on her TV. I wish I could share a happy ending to this story, but unfortunately I can't. Irene had to move into an assisted living apartment. It was downhill from there with her ongoing health issues. Her brother and sister-in-law, who had tried to help her, were left to clean out the house and try to sell it.

I could go on and on about this situation, but the point I want you to get is that it doesn't matter how large or small your cluttered space is, it is taking its toll on your emotional health which could be affecting your physical health. If you feel overwhelmed by clutter, ask for help. There are individuals and businesses that can assist you with sorting, cleaning, organizing and getting rid of the stuff you no longer need.

If you aren't at the point of being labeled a hoarder but just need to tidy things up, make a plan and start small. Begin with one drawer that has become cluttered. Keep it simple so you get it done, have a sense of accomplishment, and gain momentum. If you try to tackle the whole house at once, you will set yourself up for failure. You will give up, creating more stress and more negative thinking. Don't beat yourself up! Be kind to yourself. Remind yourself that you can do this, one step at a time. It didn't get this way overnight, so it is going to take some time to clean it up. Make a plan and follow through with it daily. There are lots of books out there on decluttering and organizing your space. Two of my favorites are *Organizing from the Inside Out* by Julie Morgenstern and *The One-Minute Organizer* by Donna Smallin. See the Appendix for more resources.

EXERCISE 5: Is there a space that needs your attention to tidy it up or to organize it? Describe that space. (Make it a small space to start with so you have success. You will continue to add spaces to your list as you clean up one space at a time.) What needs to be done in that space? Evaluate it before you dig in. Get a picture in your mind of how you want the space to look and feel. Map it out or describe it.

_____
_____
_____
_____
_____
_____
_____
_____

Remove the stuff from that space and sort it out into four piles:
- Keep
- Donate
- Sell
- Throw away

Evaluate the space while it is empty and decide what items need to go back into the space so it is being used in the best way possible. Don't try to put too much stuff back into the space or you will end up with the same cluttered mess you had before.

The items you keep have to fit one of two categories:

1. You love it (i.e. photos, treasured gifts from loved ones, mementos from special vacations or experiences, etc.).
2. You use it (i.e. anything you use on a regular basis such as dinner plates, glasses, toothpaste, shampoo, etc.).

If it doesn't fit into one of these categories, it belongs in one of the other three piles. This is where it can get tricky. Some people don't want to get rid of things because they might need them someday. This is a trap and will cause the clutter to continue. If you haven't used an item in over a year, you probably won't. It is tempting to hang onto stuff just in case, but when you really think about it, have you ever been glad you held onto stuff for years and years? Or did you come across the same stuff again and again and asked, "Why do I still have this? I haven't used it!" This has happened to me, but I'm getting better about letting things go, especially following the deaths of my father and father-in-law. My husband and I helped sort and clean out their stuff. We both decided that we don't want to leave that kind of a mess for our son to sort out when we are gone. We're doing better about getting rid of things that we were keeping just in case. I think of all of the screws and nails leftover from furniture we've put together. We keep them, but they never fit anything else. So why do we keep them? Fear of not having them if we need them. Silly, huh? I still remember a homily that Father Ed Courtney gave during Mass when I was in college. He said, "If you have something you haven't used for over a year, you are stealing from the poor." I keep this in mind when I am sorting and organizing.

EXERCISE 6: What items are you struggling to let go of? What have you kept for over a year that you haven't used? What could you donate that others could use?

_____

_____

_____

_____

_____

_____

_____

Donating items to those who are less fortunate is a practice I began with my son when he was around two or three years old. Every year before the holidays, I would have him go through his toys and pull out the ones he didn't play with anymore. Some of them were still unopened! I explained to him that there were other boys and girls who didn't have as many toys as he did and that he needed to share with them. If Santa saw all the toys he had and didn't play with, he wouldn't get any new ones. He was always happy to help me bag up the toys along with clothes that he didn't wear and help me take it all to the City Mission to help other kids. This was not only de-cluttering, but community service.

As adults, we can use this philosophy, too. When we hang on to old, useless, broken stuff that we don't love and don't use anymore, we have no room for new things. Take a look in your closet and see how many clothes you have. Take them all out of the closet and sort them into two piles – the clothes you wear regularly and the ones you haven't worn for a year or more. This includes the ones that don't fit anymore, but will fit when you lose the weight someday! Guess what? When you do lose the weight, you won't want to wear the old, out-of-style clothes. You will want to treat yourself to something new to show off your new physique! It's okay to let the old ratty clothes go! Many of them may not be suitable to donate, but need to be thrown out or recycled. The City Mission recycles old clothing and uses the money to feed and clothe the homeless. Think of the words to the song from the Disney movie *Frozen* and *Let it Go!*

EXERCISE 7: Starting with the list you made in exercise 6, get rid of seven items. Donate them, recycle them, or throw them away, but remove them from your environment. The point of this exercise is to get moving and start cleaning up your environment so you can reduce stress, be more productive and feel happier and relaxed! Do it now.

_____

_____

_____

_____

_____

How do you feel?

_____

_____

_____

_____

Once you build momentum by completing several small decluttering projects, you can move up to bigger projects. Remember the way to eat an elephant is one bite at a time. If you want to clean a whole room, start with something small and continue with bite-sized pieces until you have eaten the whole elephant. (I would never eat a real elephant, but you get the idea.) If you tackle one drawer, one table surface, one box at a time, it will get done and you will be amazed at how quickly it can happen. One strategy you may consider is to pull out a drawer and tidy it up while watching TV or to get up and go to the room where the drawer is and clean it out during commercials. If you are counting steps, this is one way to get more steps into your day and to move your body instead of sitting for a long period of time. You will be amazed at how much you can accomplish during TV commercials!

Making it Useful

Now that you have cleaned out the clutter, look at your space and decide what you need in the space that will make your life easier. This is the time to create the space you really want! You may have ideas already of how you want to use the space, but if you don't, you need to take the time right now to consider it. Make sure you have everything you need to be able to use the space for its designated purpose. Design the space so it is handy and helps you to accomplish the tasks that need to be done in that space. For example, if you are working on your home office space, decide what you need to make the space functional and comfortable, then leave out anything that doesn't belong. If you have a desk, what needs to be on the desk or in the drawers so it is handy for you? I have a computer, tape, stapler, paper clips, pens and pencils, notepads, telephone, planner and a few family pictures. I have a printer stand next to my desk that has other computer and printer supplies that I use. If you don't need it for the intended use of the space, then don't bring it into the space or you will recreate the clutter.

Julie Morgenstern describes organizing your space like a Kindergarten classroom. Everything has a place or a home so the children know where to find it when they want it and where to put it when they are done. Like or similar things go together. When I was a teacher and school counselor, I was always impressed with how well organized Kindergarten classrooms were. There were designated zones for everything. In the reading zone, there were books on shelves, chairs, tables and a rug to sit on for listening to a story read aloud. There was an area for building things so there were tubs with Legos, wooden blocks, cardboard bricks, and Lincoln Logs. The art area had easels, smocks, paints, paper, crayons, markers, colored pencils, glitter and glue. This type of organization is simple, useful and productive. When the teacher told kids it was time for art, they knew where to go and what they needed to get the job done. When it was time to clean up, they knew exactly where to put everything. If Kindergarteners can learn this skill, so can adults!

EXERCISE 8: Map out your space like a Kindergarten room. Create zones for the activities that will occur in each area. Only put supplies and items that will be used in that area. Use a large enough paper to draw your space clearly. You may use a separate map for each zone. When you are mapping out the space, take into account the furniture you will be using and measure accordingly to make sure it will fit. Remember the adage "those who fail to plan, plan to fail." If you plan well, you will be successful in creating a space that fits your needs.

Beauty

Now that you have cleaned out the clutter and have designed the space with purposeful zones, look at your space and decide what you can put into it that brings you joy and pleasure. This is where art, photos, furniture, paint, and decorative containers come in. It is tempting to buy containers before you map out your space, but wait until you know what furniture, colors and décor you will be using before you choose containers. Then you can find something that is both decorative and useful. If you buy containers before you evaluate the space and the supplies you have, you may end up with containers that aren't used or that don't fit the space. This would be a waste of time, effort, and money.

Consider the colors you want in the space. Choose something that feels right to you. For example, in my work office I want to create a sense of calm and peace so I have a wall that is slate blue. The other walls are a cream color and my loveseat is midnight navy. The carpet has muted grays, creams and a touch of slate blue. I have photographs of nature that I took on vacations mounted on canvases on the walls to add a peaceful feel. In contrast, in my scrapbooking room, I wanted vibrant bright colors to evoke my creativity so I have five walls, each painted a different color. It brings a lot of happy energy to the space when I am working on something creative. How do you want to use the space? What colors evoke the feelings you want to have while working in or enjoying that space?

What décor do you envision in your new space? Is there some art work you want to display? Is there a special photograph, painting, drawing, sculpture or heirloom you want to enjoy? Think about things you have kept in storage. Is it time to dig out some of those items that you treasured enough to keep but have never created a place where you can enjoy them on a daily basis? This is the time to gather up all of the items that you want to have in this new space and draw them on your map. Bring them into the empty space and hold them up in different areas to see where they may fit. Don't get caught up in the excitement of your clean space by bringing in too much! Keep it simple, useful and enjoyable. Whatever you do with it should bring a smile to your face!

EXERCISE 9: Finalize your map. Go back to your map and color it in with the colors you want to use. Add any decorative items that were not on your earlier map(s). Do this while you are in the room so you can look around, evaluate, measure and visualize. Don't worry about making it perfect on paper. You don't have to be a professional artist to do this exercise. Your goal is to have a plan written on paper so you can create the space you really want, will enjoy and will use for years to come.

This exercise can be done for small spaces, too. I had a client who mapped out each of his kitchen cupboards so he could organize his kitchen in a way that was useful, handy, tidy and easy to maintain. When you are organizing drawers, you may consider how you can divide the drawers into different zones and how you may create appropriate dividers. You can measure the drawers and buy plastic or wooden organizers that fit the drawers or you can make your own dividers using household items like small baskets, plastic containers, cardboard, etc. There are many ideas available in magazines, on Do it Yourself TV shows, or websites such as Pinterest.

Now is the time to take action! If you are going to paint the room, do it, then move the furniture into the room and follow your organizational map to set up the space. Take before and after pictures so you can see your progress. It is also helpful to refer back to these photos if the space begins to get untidy or cluttered (which won't happen since you will maintain your new space daily). Reward yourself for a job well done! Do something special to celebrate your success! If you did a room, invite somebody over to celebrate the space with you! Dance, sing, have a dedication ceremony, a tea party, or a picnic on the floor. If it is a de-cluttered drawer or closet, send the before and after photos to a friend so they can be a witness to your success. Treat yourself to an activity you don't normally make time for such as reading a book or magazine, painting your fingernails, taking a bubble bath, watching a movie or doing something artistic.

EXERCISE 10: What will you do to celebrate your new space? How will you reward yourself?

_____

_____

_____

_____

_____

_____

Rewarding yourself is key to ongoing success! If you don't take the time to reward yourself for accomplishing tasks or goals, you will lose momentum and find it more difficult to tackle the next goal. Our brains work on the reward system, just like those of other animals. When you train a dog, you offer a treat every time they engage in the desired behavior. Humans are the same – we want a treat. If the behavior isn't firmly in place when you begin withholding the treats, a dog will revert back to the old behavior. Without a reward, your brain operates on the "why should I cooperate with you when you didn't reward me the last time? What's in it for me?" premise. We do what works for us so there has to be a payoff somewhere to create lasting change. Trust me on this and give yourself the treat!

Chapter 16: Connecting with Nature

"We need balance. We need to balance our inner life with our outer life. Nature is always sitting there waiting to help us, but we have to do the work. Nature is probably the greatest teacher that we'll ever have . . . the earth and nature.
—*Dave Davies*

"Look deep into nature, and then you will understand everything better."
—*Albert Einstein*

We've taken a look at the space where we live and work. Now I want to look at the bigger environment and talk about the value of regularly getting outside and engaging with nature. As I experience nature, my life is put back into a healthy perspective. I feel calm and peaceful. I feel ready to go back to work or to my family feeling content and that everything is just as it should be. There is no reason to worry, no reason to swim upstream, no reason to fight the current of life. Just relax and trust that "all is well."

I just returned from an invigorating walk in our neighborhood. Although I am hot and sweaty, I feel great! I love walking outside and really appreciate it in the spring, after being cooped up during the winter months. I enjoy the sunshine, the blue sky with wispy clouds blowing overhead, the darker sky and clouds moving in as a storm moves our way, the breeze as it blows my hair and cools my sweaty face (although today it is much windier than a gentle breeze), and the fresh air that smells of spring blossoms on the trees and fresh cut grass. I like to see the green lawns and neighbors out gardening in their yards, cleaning out flower beds and tending to new flowers. I enjoy hearing the variety of birds singing and cawing to one another and seeing the geese swimming on the pond in pairs and sitting on nests as they prepare for their goslings to hatch. They honk to one another as if to give warning or to notify others that somebody has bread crumbs.

My husband created a lovely sitting area in our back yard near our garden. Attached to our cute shed that looks like a miniature house, he made a little patio with bricks and a lattice top and sides with purple clematis climbing up. It has a swing to sit and relax in. I always plan to sit out there and read or write, but I must admit I don't take advantage of it as much as I would like to. Our cat, KoKo, loves it when somebody sits out there. She likes company while she chases bugs, rolls in the grass or stalks her prey of mice, voles, or bunnies. As I sit in the swing, I can enjoy the Lincoln roses, the lilacs we transplanted from my grandmother's orchard, and the pink peonies that bloom around our house. I always feel more calm and peaceful after getting outside for a little while. It reminds me of my grandmother who told us we needed to get outside and play when we had been indoors and were getting cranky. She was right. After we played outside for a while, we were a lot happier and more pleasant to be around.

Although I know this from my life experience, why do I find myself not getting outside and connecting with nature more than I do? I can use busy-ness as an excuse, but like everyone, I have 24 hours in the day. Couldn't I find 30-60 minutes to get outside? Today I am doing laundry, dishes, baking banana bread, cleaning the office, getting caught up on my billing and writing. These chores and activities are indoor activities, but I don't have to stay inside all day to do them. The washing machine can wash clothes without me watching it. The same is true of the dryer and dishwasher. Couldn't I take some time to go out to the sitting area to write or to read? Of course I could! And I know when I do I will feel more calm, relaxed, refreshed and connected to nature

EXERCISE 1: What can you do today to get outside and connect with nature? Is there an outdoor activity that you enjoy but haven't done for a while? What about just sitting outside for 15 minutes to take in some fresh air and sunshine while you relax? Notice how you feel. Notice how your breathing changes. Notice whether or not you still feel hurried. Write in your journal about this experience.

_____

_____

_____

_____

_____

_____

After a recent storm we enjoyed the beautiful double rainbow from our deck. I took pictures which can never do it justice. Sometimes you just have to stop what you are doing and enjoy the rainbows.

EXERCISE 2: When was the last time you stopped to enjoy the rainbows or smell the roses? Has it been so long that you have forgotten? Take some time right now to stop whatever you are doing and go outside for 10-15 minutes. Use your senses to get into the experience. Take mental notes or write in your journal. What do you see, hear, smell, taste, and feel? Notice the temperature, how you are moving (if you are moving), how your body feels. Stay in the present moment and experience it fully with no thoughts about the past or future. Just be. Take time to "be" in the moment.

_____

_____

_____

_____

_____

_____

One of the things I do that keeps me grounded in the moment is to take photos of nature. When I take my camera outside with me, I am looking for nature's wonders. I look for various colors, textures, lighting and shadows. I look carefully at flowers, buds, trees, animals and butterflies. I stop, look around, listen, prepare my camera with the proper setting, and zoom in on the object of my delight. Sometimes when I look at the pictures when I get home, I not only can recall the image, but I recall the feelings of wonder, awe and peacefulness that I felt when I took the pictures.

EXERCISE 3: Your assignment is to go outside with a sense of wonder and awe. If you like to draw, take art supplies with you so you can draw or paint. If you like photography, take your camera. If you have trouble slowing down and enjoying nature, take a child or a pet with you. They are great at noticing all of the little wonders of nature that adults tend to overlook. Have them show you what they see. Get down to their level to see it from their vantage point. Observe and take note as a scientist does. Report your findings to another person or in your journal.

_____

_____

_____

_____

_____

_____

_____

_____

_____

_____

"I believe as human beings we are out of balance, out of synch with the earth."
—Kevin Richardson

Chapter 17: Giving Back

"I don't know what your destiny will be, but one thing I do know: the only ones among you who will be really happy are those who have sought and found how to serve."
—*Albert Schweitzer*

Giving back to the world is key in helping you feel useful and grateful for all that you have. This is an important piece in creating your balanced life. The main point of this chapter is to consider how to give back to others. It is one thing to give to family and friends, but is quite different to give to others, sometimes people we don't know, have never met and never will. If you consider the world as our community and you recognize that we are all connected, it makes sense to help others. It makes the world a better place for all of us.

I had a 33-year-old single client that I will call Hannah. She had recently moved to town for a job and wanted to meet other people. She had a strong desire to get involved in community service so we created a list of ideas that matched her values and goals. She contacted people that she thought may have information on some of the organizations she was interested in. I shared resources and names that I thought could help her. She decided to meet with the leader of one of the groups to evaluate if it met her needs. If it did, she would continue. If not, she would drop it and try something different. She found an organization that helped women and children. She reported back that she liked the group and the work they did so she was planning to try them out for a while.

I encourage you to think like Hannah and find a place where you can invest in your community. Let's start with a simple assessment.

Community covers a lot of different areas. For the purposes of this chapter, consider all of the activities in which you are involved with people outside of your family and close friends. This would include all organizations in which you are involved, serve, volunteer, or otherwise participate. These may be professional organizations, service organizations, school activities, sporting activities, church/synagogue/temple activities, networking organizations, etc. How do you serve others?

Service to others does not have to be on a grand scale. It can be helping your neighbor, visiting someone in a nursing home, or assisting a few people with specific needs. There are many organizations who would love to have volunteers as they can't operate without the help. Consider what your interests are, who could benefit from your help, the time you have available, and the location. Choose something that you would enjoy supporting. You may choose to do it one time or you may choose an ongoing commitment. Do you like to help animals? Consider the animal shelter, or a rescue organization. Do you prefer to work alone in your service? What about shelving books or preparing them for mailing by volunteering at the library? If you don't have a lot of time but would prefer to help once a year, what about helping with a community event that relies on volunteers?

My point is, there are numerous ways to serve others. My husband donates blood at the Community Blood Bank. I clean trash off the bike trail and am involved in a number of organizations. If you are having difficulty thinking of ideas to serve others, here are a few to get you started:

    A. Professional Organizations
    B. Service Organizations (Lions Club, Kiwanis Club, Shriners, Optimists Club, etc.)
    C. Schools
    D. Church, Synagogue, Temple, etc.
    E. Hospitals
    F. Nursing Homes
    G. Animal Shelters
    H. Libraries
    I. Literacy Volunteers

J. Big Brothers/Big Sisters, Teammates or other groups that encourage mentorship with children and teens
K. Sporting event volunteers
L. Special events in your area (such as special guests, entertainment, fairs, etc.)
M. Political parties
N. Meals on Wheels
O. Habitat for Humanity
P. Ecology or environmental groups
Q. Animal rescue or preservation groups

EXERCISE 1: List the community organizations that you are already a part of.

_____

_____

_____

_____

_____

_____

_____

_____

Everybody is busy. We live in a busy world with constant access to information, technology and activity that will suck up all of our time like the world's most powerful vacuum cleaner . . . if we let it. We want to have the benefits of various organizations, but don't feel like we have the time to devote to volunteering to help keep them going. It is easy to allow others to do the work for the majority to get the benefit. The problem with this is that people burn out and good organizations die. When we don't step up and help out, we all miss out on an opportunity to grow and to learn. I am a member of a number of organizations and was just installed as an officer in the Toastmasters club again after taking a number of years off. Others took over when I was otherwise engaged, so I figured it is time for me to shoulder the burden again.

Earlier in this book, I talked about the importance of managing your time and saying no to the organizations and projects that don't feel right or that don't excite you. This doesn't mean to say no to everything! If you have depleted your energy by saying yes to too many things, it is important to take time to refill your bucket and to evaluate what is most meaningful to you. Go back to your balance assessment in chapter 2 and use it to help you decide where you may enjoy getting involved.

For example, if family is at the top of your list, as it was for me, you may choose to volunteer at your child's school. Schools often need volunteers and would gladly accept your help. Volunteering at my son's school enhanced my life and my values of family and education, so it was a productive way to serve my community. I was able to offer my time, experience and expertise to help other parents' children as well as to set an example for my son.

When my son was seven or eight years old, we volunteered to help run a game booth at the church Bazaar. There were two other boys that volunteered to help so my son got to know two other kids and they all benefitted from helping others—especially in teaching the younger children how to play the game and offering them prizes. The work seemed like fun and our shift passed quickly. It was a great opportunity to model helping others with no expectation of getting anything in return.

EXERCISE 2: Consider your community service. If you are not currently involved in any organizations, are there any that you have considered joining but felt like you were too busy to join in the past? If you haven't considered it, is there an organization that aligns with an interest or passion you have that would benefit from your help? If you are unsure, research different organizations and see how and where you may enjoy serving others in a way that feels right to you. List organizations that you will research this week. What are the benefits of serving others?

_____

_____

_____

_____

_____

_____

_____

_____

EXERCISE 3: After you serve others, how do you feel?

_____

_____

_____

_____

_____

_____

I had a professor who said that if you want to help somebody who is depressed, there are 10 things you can tell them they need to do:

- Number 1 – do something for somebody else.
- Number 2 – do something for somebody else.
- Number 3 – do something for somebody else.
- Etc.

You get the idea. When you help others, you remove the focus from yourself and your problems. You change your focus to others, which allows you to put your own problems into perspective. You realize all of the blessings you have in your life compared to those who are having a more difficult time than you are. You become more appreciative and grateful. You feel good about helping others and contributing to the world. In helping others, you are helping bring balance within yourself as well as to the universe.

"You must be the change you wish to see in the world."
—Mahatma Ghandi

Chapter 18: Finding Meaning and Purpose

"For the meaning of life differs from man to man, from day to day and from hour to hour. What matters, therefore, is not the meaning of life in general but rather the specific meaning of a person's life at a given moment."
—*Viktor E. Frankl*

"'The Wizard of Oz' is my favorite. It explains what life on this planet is about. Although Dorothy reaches Oz, she finds she had what she needed to go back to Kansas all along, but the Good Witch tells her that she had to learn it for herself. All of the answers to the meaning of life are there."
—*RuPaul*

What is the meaning of life? This is a great philosophical question that has received much attention, but to which nobody has the great answer. There are comic strips that show a thin elderly man with a long white beard sitting on the top of a mountain, or better yet, floating above it. He is the wise sage and he awaits seekers who ask him this question. There is always some joke offered in response, but if we are honest with ourselves, we are hoping to get a real answer. I hope you find some useful answers in the quotations for this chapter.

Viktor Frankl's book, *Man's Search for Meaning*, was first published in Austria in 1946. It has been revised, updated and reprinted numerous times and has sold millions of copies. It is an

149

amazing story of how Frankl not only survived life in Nazi concentration camps after his whole family was murdered, but how he was able to find meaning in the suffering and helped others to thrive. He founded the Third Viennese School of Psychotherapy based on his theory of logotherapy, which comes from his belief that "man's primary motivational force is his search for meaning". I encourage you to check out this book as it is one you won't forget.

I don't want to get into the clinical aspects of logotherapy and Frankl's teachings but this quotation from *Man's Search for Meaning* sums it up to some degree: "One should not search for an abstract meaning of life. Everyone has his own specific vocation or mission in life to carry out a concrete assignment which demands fulfillment. Therein he cannot be replaced, nor can his life be repeated. Thus, everyone's task is as unique as is his specific opportunity to implement it."

This is the way I explain it to my clients: We are all sent here for a reason. Nobody is here by accident. It is up to each one of us to figure out our purpose. Those answers were planted inside each one of us before we were sent here and they are still there. Sometimes they get covered up with lots of the junk that happens to us throughout our lives. It may seem like those answers are gone, but they are not. We just have to dig down through the muck to get to them. It is my job to help you dig down. I don't have your answers. You have them, deep inside. Nobody else can tell you what they are because you are the only one who has access to them.

I believe the answers are planted in your heart. You know when something feels right or not. As I explained in the section about Intuition in the chapter on Spirituality, you have an inner compass. This compass directs you toward your purpose. When you feel lost, it is because you are not in tune with your compass and you have lost direction. This is when you make bad choices, get depressed and feel bad about yourself. Once you clear out the interference, your compass is free to point you in the right direction. You just have to follow it. When you do, you will find your life is in flow and everything becomes easier.

EXERCISE 1: Take time to check in with yourself. Get quiet, close your eyes and ask yourself, "What do I really want?" Keep asking this question until you begin hearing an answer. Where is your inner compass directing you to go? Do you have a clear direction or are you lost in a boat on the sea of life without a rudder or an oar? If you can see where you are supposed to go, what obstacles are preventing you from getting to your destination? If you can't see where you are going, how can you clear out the interference to get your compass in working order? What can you do to start getting direction so you can navigate? You may find it useful to look back at your responses to previous exercises.

_____

_____

_____

_____

_____

_____

_____

_____

_____

_____

_____

EXERCISE 2: What is your purpose in this moment? What meaning can you derive from quiet introspection? Take some time to meditate on the present moment. Feel the compass pointing you in the right direction. When you are ready, take a few minutes to write about your experience.

_____

_____

_____

_____

_____

_____

_____

_____

_____

_____

_____

_____
_____
_____
_____
_____
_____
_____
_____
_____
_____
_____
_____
_____
_____
_____
_____
_____
_____
_____
_____
_____
_____
_____
_____
_____

Dreams

"Go confidently in the direction of your dream! Live the life
you've imagined. As you simplify your life, the laws of the universe
will be simpler."
—*Henry David Thoreau*

*"The biggest adventure you can take is to live the life
of your dreams."*
—*Oprah Winfrey*

Dream, Plan, Achieve is the tagline for my life coaching business. I chose these three words because they set the stage for reaching goals which is the basis for life coaching. I began with the idea of dreaming because so many people have no idea what they want to do to find joy and meaning in their lives.

If we are going to explore dreaming it helps to define it.

Dream, noun, often attributive \'drēm\

> : a series of thoughts, visions or feelings that happen during sleep
>
> : an idea or vision that is created in your imagination and that is not real
>
> : something that you have wanted very much to do, be, or have for a long time

In this chapter, I want to focus on the third definition, although we may use aspects of the first two definitions to derive ideas for the third.

Many people are accused of being dreamers, an insult meant to bring them back down to earth, to get their head out of the clouds, but do they really need to stop dreaming? Einstein credits many of his greatest ideas to dreaming at night and recalling the dreams. Stephen King attributes his dreams as the basis of his 2001 novel turned film *Dreamcatcher*. Surrealist painter Salvador Dali called many of his works "hand-painted dream photographs". My favorite Dali work, "Persistence of Memory," shows images of melting clocks inspired from an actual dream. Paul McCartney woke from a dream in 1964 with the melody for "Yesterday" in his head. Edgar Allan Poe said nightmares and dreams often inspired his short stories and poems. Knowing that so many successful people were dreamers who took action on their dreams is a reminder that we can also bring our dreams into reality.

Children know how to dream and express this in their imaginary play. They create characters, stories and actions that adults may think are unrealistic, but this doesn't stop them from having fun and bringing their dreams or fantasies into reality. Unfortunately, as children mature, they often lose this ability to create and act out their dreams. The ones who are reluctant to let go of this ability are labeled immature and are encouraged to grow up, meaning "stop fantasizing and get to work!" They are told their dreams are unrealistic and they need to change their dreams so they can make a living. Maybe you have noticed that there are some young people who kept dreaming and are making a good living as a result.

EXERCISE 3: Recall your childhood. What did you dream about? How did you use your imagination? When did you stop? Who or what influenced you to stop?

_____

_____

_____

_____

_____

What would you do if you were allowed to dream and didn't have to make a living by being realistic?

_____

_____

_____

_____

_____

How would your life be different if you hadn't bought into the naysayers and had believed in your dream and your ability to make it come true?

_____

_____

_____

_____

_____

_____

If time and money were not factors and you could do whatever you wanted to do, what would you do?

_____
_____
_____
_____
_____
_____

What career would feel easy, effortless and fun? What would you do in your personal life?

_____
_____
_____
_____
_____
_____

If you haven't thought about these possibilities, how do you feel realizing that it is possible to have a career and life that you love and it doesn't have to be difficult?

_____
_____
_____

"So how do I do that?" you ask. The **first step** to discover your purpose and passion in life is to go back to the exercise in Chapter 2 and list four or five of your core values. According to life coach, Heather Rem in her book, _Inspiration to Realization_, "values are things you feel connected to; they allow you to feel peaceful inside, and truly alive". Here are a few examples: adventure, daring, honesty, contribution, teaching, creativity, discovery, learning, experience, leadership, feeling, inspiring, mastery, excelling, pleasure, fun, relating to others, connection, sensitivity, being supportive, spirituality, uplift, winning, accomplishing, acquiring, etc.

EXERCISE 4: Write down four or five of your core values.

_____

_____

_____

_____

_____

The **second step** is to examine your life and see where your values currently show up and how. Are you living your life according to your values? If not, what can you do to honor your values and orient your life around them?

EXERCISE 5: List the areas in your life where you are living by your values.

_____

_____

_____

_____

What can you do to honor your values and orient your life around those areas?

_____

_____

_____

_____

The **third step** is to make a list of your past jobs and the parts that felt most right. What excited you most? What felt effortless? What was fun?

_____

_____

_____

_____

_____

The **fourth step** is to consider what you like to do in your free time. Do you have a hobby or interest that you could get paid for? Here are a few examples: photography, making crafts, sewing, cooking, gardening, writing music or playing an instrument, teaching people how to use computer programs, training dogs, etc.

_____
_____
_____
_____
_____
_____
_____
_____

The **fifth step** is to take a look at your childhood. What did you enjoy doing? What did you want to be when you grew up? Do these dreams match your values?

_____
_____
_____
_____
_____
_____
_____
_____

This could be the key to a passion that you had but put aside. How can you make room in your life for a passion you once had?

_____
_____
_____
_____
_____

You will find a few quotations about dreaming in Appendix C. Choose one or two and post them where you can see them daily to inspire you to keep dreaming.

"All our dreams can come true, if we have the courage to pursue them."
—Walt Disney

"So many of our dreams at first seem impossible, then they seem improbable, and then, when we summon the will, they soon become inevitable."
—Christopher Reeve

"Twenty years from now you will be more disappointed by the things that you didn't do than by the ones you did do. So throw off the bowlines. Sail away from the safe harbor. Catch the trade winds in your sails. Explore. Dream. Discover."
—Mark Twain

We are all happier when we follow our dreams, make a plan and achieve our goals and dreams. When we use our values to guide us, we feel at peace, knowing we are following a life path with ease, excitement and fun. We have briefly looked at our dreams and how to make them come true.

It's never too late to make your dreams come true. Start today! Remember my business motto: Dream, Plan, Achieve!

Chapter 19: Living in Balance

"The best and safest thing is to keep a balance in your life, acknowledge the great powers around us and in us. If you can do that, and live that way, you are really a wise man."
—Euripedes

Creating a balanced life is not always easy, but is essential to happiness and fulfillment. Balance is not the same for any two people as we are all different with different strengths, needs, abilities and preferences. You will continue to re-evaluate and make adjustments to fine tune your life and to adjust to a new balance throughout the stages of your life's journey. Don't compare your life balance formula to anyone else's as you have your own answers about what works best for you.

Use the assessment to re-balance your life whenever you are feeling a shift that seems to be throwing you off-balance. Remind yourself of your values, which things are non-negotiable in maintaining your sense of balance and which things you need to let go of, temporarily or permanently. Use what you have learned about yourself from the exercises in this book to maintain an even keel. The boat may rock, but it doesn't have to tip over leaving you gasping for air as you try not to drown.

Balance is all about managing time efficiently to incorporate all the important aspects of your life. If you don't schedule in all aspects of your life, there will be imbalance. Sometimes there is a certain area that requires more focused energy, which means that you have to let go of something else for a time. This doesn't mean it is a permanent change, so don't get too attached. The perfect balance is constantly shifting and you will continually adjust your sails.

I have continually tweaked to find balance throughout my life and I can assure you that it is much different now than it has been at any other stage of my life. I will continue to adjust to deal with obstacles, changing currents, and strong winds that try to blow me off course, and so will you. You have the tools to navigate your life balance. Use your inner compass and trust in your inner wisdom. You have a strong sense of direction so don't let somebody else take over and steer your boat. You are the captain of your ship. Keep it balanced and upright. Enjoy your life's journey.

About the Author

Kolleen Meyer-Krikac, M.S. Ed., is a Licensed Professional Counselor, National Certified Counselor, Licensed Mental Health Practitioner and Certified Life Coach in private practice with her business, Balanced Life, in Lincoln, Nebraska. She uses her skills as a former teacher when she offers workshops, trainings, webinars, online courses, and small group coaching. She also speaks to organizations on a variety of topics related to creating balance, achieving goals and finding meaning. She is a member of a number of professional organizations including ACA (American Counseling Association), APPT (Association of Private Practice Therapists), and NBCC (National Board for Certified Counselors). Kolleen enjoys public speaking and is a member of Toastmasters International.

To invite Kolleen to speak, consult, or provide a workshop, please contact her through her website: www.balanced-life.us You can also sign up for her newsletter on her website.

Email: kolleen@balanced-life.us

Phone: 402-499-5547

Facebook Page: kolleenmeyerkrikacauthor/

Kolleen's motto is "Dream, Plan, Achieve." Stop making excuses and begin moving toward the dreams you have put on the back burner.

Appendices

Appendix A: Charts and Worksheets
  Self-Assessment
  Time Management Chart
  Contract with Yourself
  Urgent/Important Chart
  High Energy/Low Energy Time Chart
Appendix B: References
Appendix C: Resources

Appendix A: Charts and Worksheets

Self-Assessment

	Order of Importance	How I Spend My Time	Needs Most Attention
Self Care/ Health			
Family			
Friends/Social			
Work			
Finances			
Spirituality			
Fun			
Education			
Environment/ Surroundings			
Community			
Purpose/Meaning			

Time Management Chart

Time	Sunday	Monday	Tuesday
6-7 a.m.			
7-8 a.m.			
8-9 a.m.			
9-10 a.m.			
10-11 a.m.			
11 a.m.- 12 p.m.			
12-1 p.m.			
1-2 p.m.			
2-3 p.m.			
3-4 p.m.			
4-5 p.m.			
5-6 p.m.			
6-7 p.m.			
7-8 p.m.			
8-9 p.m.			
9-10 p.m.			
10-11 p.m.			
11 p.m.– 12 a.m.			

Time Management Chart			
Wednesday	Thursday	Friday	Saturday

Contract with Yourself

I, _____, am committing myself to the follow-through and completion of the following goal:

Beginning on (date) _____, I (What are you going to do? Be specific.)

_____

_____

_____

_____by

(completion date) _____

I will ask _____ to be my accountability partner to hold me to the follow-through and completion of this goal. We will meet (how often, how long and where?) _____

_____

_____

_____I

will reward myself for completing small steps with _____

_____

_____

_____

Upon completion of this goal, I will celebrate by _____

_____

_____

_____

Signed by _____

Date_____

Accountability Partner(s) Signature(s) _____

_____

Date _____

Accountability Partner(s) Signature(s) _____

_____

Date _____

Urgent/Important Chart

	IMPORTANT	NOT IMPORTANT
URGENT		
NOT URGENT		

High Energy/Low Energy Time Chart

Time	Sunday	Monday	Tuesday
6-7 a.m.			
7-8 a.m.			
8-9 a.m.			
9-10 a.m.			
10-11 a.m.			
11 a.m.- 12			
12-1 p.m.			
1-2 p.m.			
2-3 p.m.			
3-4 p.m.			
4-5 p.m.			

High Energy/Low Energy Time Chart

Wednesday	Thursday	Friday	Saturday

Appendix B: References

References

Chapter 4
Exercises Adapted from *Take Time for Your Life* Cheryl Richardson.
Richardson, Cheryl, *Take Time for Your Life* (New York: Broadway
Books, 1998), Pages 83-85, 153-155

Chapter 5
http://whyquit.com/whyquit/A_Benefits_Time_Table.html

Chapter 9
Adams, Susan. "Unhappy Employees Outnumber Happy Ones by
Two to One Worldwide," *Forbes Magazine* , Oct. 10, 2013

Sullivan, Bob and Hugh Thompson, ,"Brain, Interrupted." *New York
Times Sunday Review, May 3, 2013,*
https://www.nytimes.com/2013/05/05/opinion/sunday/a-focus-on-
distraction.html?mwrsm=Emai)

Songwriters: Richard M. Sherman / Robert B. Sherman
A Spoonful of Sugar lyrics © Walt Disney Music Company

Chapter 10
Franklin, Ben. "Advice to a Young Tradesman.
www.quotes.yourdictionary.com. Emphasizes the importance of this
concept to business people and entrepreneurs. He further explained
that capable people lose money by not working and by spending it

while not working so wasting time wastes money in two ways: 1. By not earning and 2. By spending. If you want to stay in business, don't squander opportunities and money.

"Money doesn't grow on trees." Old financial proverb. It is a saying that is "said to warn someone to be careful how much money they spend, because there is only a limited amount.")

Herbert, George. *Outlandish Proverbs,* circa 1633. "A penny saved is a penny earned." Herbert's version, "A penny spar'd is twice got." means "it is as useful to save money that you already have as it is to earn more." – found online at *www.phrases.org.uk)*

Chapter 11
Shapiro, Rabbi Rami. *"What is the Difference Between Religion and Spirituality?* spiritualityhealth.com, May-June 2012.

Shapiro. *"The Difference Between Spirituality and Religion?"* Dated July-August 2009

Niebuhrm Reinhold. "The Serenity Prayer", (1892-1971),

Cameron, Julia, *The Artist's Way* (New York: Tarcher/Putnam Books, 1992), Pages 9-24

Winfrey, Oprah & Deepak Chopra "21-Day Meditation Experiences," *chopracentermeditation.com.*

Pacifica phone app

Chapter 19
Frankl, Viktor, *Man's Search for Meaning,* (Boston, MA: Beacon Press, 1959, 1962, 1984) First published in Austria in 1946, under the title *Ein Psycholog erlebt das Konzentrationslager.*

Rem, Heather, *Inspiration to Realization,* (Los Angeles, CA: Love Your Life, 2004)

Appendix C: Resources

Resources

Chapter 4
Richardson, Cheryl, *Take Time for Your Life* (New York: Broadway Books, 1998)

Richardson, Cheryl, *Life Makeovers* (New York: Broadway Books, 2000)

Chapter 6
Lashier, Kathy, *Tell Me Your Memories Grandpa* (ISBN: 978-1563830389) 1992

Lashier, Kathy, *Tell Me Your Memories Grandma* (ISBN-13: 978-1563830372) 1992

Chapter 11
Super Soul Sunday on Oprah's OWN network

Joel Osteen TV show

Wayne Dyer on Hay House Radio Podcast

Chapter 12
Welter, Paul Ed.D., *Learning from Children*, (Wheaton, Illinois: Tyndale House Publishers, Inc., 1984)
Welter, Paul, Radio show entitled *Learning from Children*

Chapter 15
Morgenstern, Julie, *Organizing from the Inside Out* (New York: Henry Holt and Company, 1998)

Smallin, Donna, *The One-Minute Organizer* (North Adams, Massachusetts: Storey Publishing, 2004)

Chapter 20
Quotations on Dreams:

> *"The world needs dreamers and the world needs doers. But above all, the world needs dreamers who do."*
> **Sarah Ban Breathnach**

> *"All our dreams can come true, if we have the courage to pursue them."*
> **Walt Disney**

> *"To accomplish great things, we must not only act, but also dream; not only plan, but also believe."*
> **Anatole France**

> *"Nothing happens unless first a dream."*
> **~Carl Sandburg**

> *"So many of our dreams at first seem impossible, then they seem improbable, and then, when we summon the will, they soon become inevitable."*
> **Christopher Reeve**

> *"Twenty years from now you will be more disappointed by the things that you didn't do than by the ones you did do. So throw off the bowlines. Sail away from the safe harbor. Catch the trade winds in your sails. Explore. Dream. Discover."*
> **~Mark Twain**

"If one advances confidently in the direction of his dreams, and endeavors to live the life which he has imagined, he will meet with a success unexpected in common hours."
Henry David Thoreau

"If you take responsibility for yourself you will develop a hunger to accomplish your dreams."
Les Brown

"You have to dream before your dreams can come true."
Abdul Kalam

"Do all you can to make your dreams come true."
Joel Osteen

68196350R00112

Made in the USA
Lexington, KY
05 October 2017